I like to believe that I was born near Sedona ~~because I am meant to~~ work with the Vortices. Those who take the time to read this book will find that I have a native understanding of the subject which sets me apart from other teachers.

At the time of this writing, this is the most in-depth and detailed book on this subject. I do not, however, claim to know all there is to know about the Vortices, or Earth energy. It is important to understand that all of us are taking part in this great adventure together. I am merely the one that the Earth has chosen to gather this information.

The Vortex phenomenon is not a passing fad. It is instead one of the signs that the Human Race is developing planetary consciousness and re-discovering its spiritual nature. We are the children of the Earth, and we have traditionally sought inspiration and healing in places where the Spirit of the Earth is strong: It is natural for us to seek out Power Spots: as modern Americans we are merely re-discovering the ancient ways.

The call of the Earth has long been ignored, but within our hearts it has never been forgotten. People are drawn to Sedona because they instinctively know that they need the Earth's boost to re-awaken their mystical connection with the Earth, and the Universe itself.

Vortices can supply such a boost. Simply stated, a Vortex is a place where the energy of the Earth is strong. By learning how to "tune in" to this energy we can increase our natural psychic abilities.

The Vortex phenomenon can be understood in scientific, spiritual, or metaphysical terms:

Scientific types will be happy to know that "Earth Energy" is not an intangible metaphysical substance. Earth energy is the electromagnetic field of the Earth. NASA research has proven that our Central Nervous Systems are "tuned" to an "Earth Wave" (natural radio wave which is produced by the Earth) which oscillates at between 7-8 cycles per second.

The alpha brain wave state, which is associated with deep relaxation, meditation, and certain forms of paranormal psychic experiences, also occurs between 7-8 cycles per second.

This means that when our brain waves are at the same frequency as the Earth wave we have tuned in to what could metaphorically be called the "heartbeat of the Mother." It is at this time that we may (by luck or training) enter an altered state of consciousness which may allow us to have the kind of experience that most people just read about.

So much for scientific explanations. There is only so much that can be explained logically. As those who are in a position to know will tell you, there is also Spirit. The Universe is Spirit, our planet is Spirit, and all upon it are Spirit.

Spirit is intelligent power.

1

SEDONA POWER SPOT, VORTEX AND MEDICINE WHEEL GUIDE

by
RICHARD DANNELLEY

Published by Richard Dannelley
in cooperation with the Vortex Society, Sedona, Arizona.
and the Heart of Light Ojai, California.

Printed in the USA by Light Technology, Sedona, Arizona.

Address all correspondence to:
Richard Dannelley in care of the Vortex Society,
p.o. box 948
Sedona Arizona 86336

Book design, graphics, cover, and mandala by Richard Dannelley

Photography Richard Dannelley

10 9 8 7 6 5 4

⊕ SEDONA POWER SPOT, VORTEX ⊕
AND MEDICINE WHEEL GUIDE

"This we know. The Earth does not belong to man; man belongs to the Earth. All things are connected like the blood of one family. Whatever befalls the Earth, befalls children of the Earth. Man did not weave the web of life, he is merely a strand in it. Whatever he does to the web, he does to himself."

Chief Seattle

TABLE OF CONTENTS

SECTION FIVE:
NOTES ON BEING A SPIRITUAL WARRIOR

SECTION SIX:
MEDITATIONS FOR DEVELOPING PSYCHIC ABILITIES

SECTION SEVEN:
VORTEX MYTHOLOGY

SECTION EIGHT:
THE WAY OF THE MEDICINE WHEEL

* These Sections Contain Key Information About Vortex Energy

MAPS

⊕ THE VORTEX SOCIETY ⊕

Perhaps the best way to guarantee that we will always have the right to visit the Vortices is to establish an organization. The Vortex society is dedicated to the study of the Vortex phenomenon, making information about the Vortices available, and preserving our right to visit the Vortices.

The four "major Vortices" are on Forest Service land, but this does not mean that we will always be given free access to them. In fact, unless the metaphysical community starts taking steps now, to protect our rights, we may someday be faced with restrictions which will be designed to keep us off, and out, of these places. (Much to the delight of the local religious fundamentalists and many real estate developers.)

The United States Forest Services is charged with "taking care of the land." Some factions within the Forest Service believe that the best way to take care of the land is to keep people off of it!

Local Forest Service officials have already admitted that they can foresee the day when they may "have to" close both Boynton Canyon and Bell Rock to public access. The reasons which will be given will be that overuse has disturbed the topsoil and damaged plantlife to the point where "it simply needs a rest."

Do not think this can not happen: Over the years every American has seen even more outrageous things than this occur, so it important for us to be aware of these things, and act now to protect our rights.

First, we have to make sure that the establishment understands that we visit the Vortices for spiritual reasons; thus helping us establish our right to visit them under our constitutionally guaranteed right to freedom of religion.

Secondly, we have to take care of the natural features of these places so the Forest Service cannot say that we are damaging them. This means staying on the trail, and being careful not to damage plants. (Remember that Sedona's plantlife is fragile; merely brushing against bushes can break them.) Avoid walking on small plants such as weeds and grasses; they help hold the soil. And please leave all flowers on their plants so that they can have a chance to produce seeds, and the next generation of beautiful flowers.

In the next few years we are going to see some trail improvements around the Vortex areas which will probably be built by volunteer labor. Please respect any barriers which have been erected to close off "side trails." Much of the erosion damage around the Vortex areas is caused by these side trails which spiderweb the landscape but lead to no particular place.

We know that many people visit the Vortices seeking spiritual insight, and that the Vortices have taken on the status of religious shrines. Therefore, we can claim access to the Vortices under our constitutionally guaranteed right to religious freedom. This means that we have the right to visit the Vortices to meditate, pray, and hold ceremonies.

⊕ THE VORTEX SOCIETY ⊕

The Vortex Society is a Universalist spiritual organization that respects the inner truth of all religions. Members of the Vortex Society recognize the fact that Sedona is sacred Earth, and that the energies of her Vortices and other Power Spots are of great value to those who seek spiritual renewal and guidance.

THE VORTEX SOCIETY NEWSLETTER

If you are planning a trip to Sedona and you would like a guide to help you explore some of the techniques in this book or if you would like a healing or high-level transformational energy work, please contact me in advance, through the mail. (There may be a card with my phone number inserted into this book.)

I do read all of my mail, and I often receive very nice letters that truly brighten my days. Unfortunately, because of the time it would require, I am not able to answer most of my mail. Because of this, I offer a single-issue newsletter to all who ask to join the Vortex Society and donate five dollars or more to help defray printing, postage and handling costs.

The newsletter will include information on classes or other events and a phone number where I can be contacted.

To receive at least one newsletter, send me a card with the following words:
I would like to join the Vortex Society. I support open access to public lands and I oppose Forest Service land trades in the Sedona area.

Please include a five dollar donation.

The Vortex Society
P.O. Box 948, Sedona, Az. 86339

LOOK FOR BOOK TWO OF THE SEDONA SERIES:

THE SEDONA UFO CONNECTION AND
PLANETARY ASCENSION GUIDE

Ask for it at your local bookstore. Distributed by New Leaf, DeVorss, Bookpeople, Baker and Taylor. Or fourteen dollars, postpaid, from the Vortex Society.

This is is not a lengthy book. In fact, it contains only about a hundred pages of text. Those who read these pages will find that they contain a great deal of information. Very few words have been wasted. The average reader should be able to read this book in four to six hours.

This is a self published book, produced without the aid of a professional editor or the financial backing and production help of a publishing house. I ask that the reader overlook any minor flaws this book may contain, recognizing instead the value of the material presented.

The word "Vortexes" does not exist in the King's English. Webster's dictionary (of American English) allows for two plural forms of the word "Vortex": Vortices and Vortexes. I prefer the word Vortices for two reasons. One is that "Vortexes" sounds like bad English to me (as it is), the other is because "Vortexes" reminds me of the word "Texas," which is not a state of enlightenment.

Many people are under the impression that "Page Bryant discovered the Vortexes." This is only partially true. She was indeed the first person to use (and misuse) the word Vortex to describe the mysterious Power Spots of Sedona. And she is rightfully credited with being the first to bring forth the information that defined these Power Spots. She is, however, definitely not the first person to either notice the Power of the red rocks or work with it.

We know that the Indians who came here before us regarded Sedona as a sacred place long before the first White settlers arrived. And in fact, modern spiritual seekers have been drawn to Sedona to experience her special energies since at least as early the mid to late fifties... (The Chapel of the Holy Cross was built in 1955-56.)

The person who should be credited with bringing the mysterious Power of Sedona into the group consciousness is Dick Sutphen, who like many others, was drawn here to experience Sedona's energies and grow. Mr. Sutphen has never claimed to have discovered the Power Spots of Sedona. He freely admits that he learned of the strange Power of the place which we now call the Airport Vortex from an acquaintance.

As I cast my memory back in time, I distinctly remember hearing Mr. Sutphen on the Phoenix area radio station KDKB in 1976 or '77 speaking about the "mysterious power spot" near the Sedona airport. (This is when I became interested in this subject.)

Dick Sutphen published information about the Airport Vortex in 1978 in his book, Past Lives Future Loves. During that period of time he also gave talks at his seminars in the Phoenix area about the mysterious energies of both the Airport Vortex and Bell Rock. In 1980 he spoke on this subject at one of his seminars in Scottsdale, Arizona, at which Page Bryant appeared as a guest speaker.

Mr. Sutphen's lecture seems to be what got Page interested in Sedona, because three months later she channeled the information about the Vortices which has inspired so many people. She identified Boynton Canyon and Cathedral Rock as major Power Spots, and gave us valuable clues about the nature of the energies we encounter at these places.

Page Bryant's channeling is an excellent example of how a Human Being can "tune in" to the energy of Spirit and receive information. At the time of this writing she is available for readings through one of our local bookstores.

Much of the information about the geological origins of the Sedona Vortices was given to me by my friend and associate, Mr. John Armbruster. John has a master of science degree in geology, and has studied the geology of Sedona in relation to the Vortices since 1987. As far as I know, Mr. Armbruster originated the theory that the energy of the Vortices emerges from the inner Earth via the Oak Creek fault, and that it is borne to the surface through iron bearing veins of basalt. (This theory is based upon accepted geological principles.)

John may be the first to have noticed that the magnetic Vortex at Cathedral Rock is centered around a large basalt vein. It was this discovery which led him to the realization that the magnetic energy of the Vortices is due to the presence of veins of iron bearing basalt in the red rocks. (He calls 'em "basalt intrusions.")

It is important to note that life as we know it would be impossible without electromagnetic energy. This is not new age hocus pocus; it is scientific fact. As much as I would like include an entire section in this book about this subject, I think it is more appropriate to suggest that those who are interested in the scientific aspect of electromagnetism in relation to the Human body should write to me in care of the Vortex Society. When I receive your letter I will send you a newsletter that you will find most interesting...

I would like to mention that the latest research suggests that many types of disease (including AIDS) can be cured with energies similar to radio waves. It is unfortunate that due to the unwillingness of the scientific establishment to accept new ideas which do not fit their pre-conceived concepts "about how things work," it may be years before electromagnetic therapy is used in hospitals. Fortunately certain types of electromagnetic therapy devices may now be purchased for self treatment.

Thanks to Dick, Page, and John, I have been able to put together the first detailed explanation of the Vortex phenomenon.

I would also like to thank evolutionary agents: Juan, Carlos, Jose, Tim, and Anton, Queen Karen (my lover and Earth contact), Herb Dorsey, Ken Pinyan, Ms. Crystal Waters, my friends at the Crystal Castle, Dirk van Dijk and Jackie at the Eye of the Vortex, my friends at the Sedona Public Library, and the Popcorn Goddess, patron saint of starving artists.

I thank the Great Spirit for the gift of consciousness.

Richard Dannelley

GEOMANCY , SHAMANISM, AND THE EVOLUTION OF PLANETARY CONSCIOUSNESS

This group of rock spires stands just to the east of the "Y" — the intersection of highways 179 and 89A. This formation is a good example of the complex forms found in the Sedona landscape.

GEOMANCY: THE SPIRIT OF THE EARTH
⊕ AND THE WEB OF LIFE ⊕

Wise men, philosophers, astronomers, and physicists know that everything throughout the Universe is moving in a balanced harmonious dance of energy. The art and science of geomancy helps us learn to become aware of these Universal energies as they are experienced upon the Planet Earth.

The literal meaning of the word geomancy is; to "divine" the Earth Spirit. To "divine" is to seek understanding or knowledge through intuition. The accepted definition of geomancy, according to most modern English dictionaries is: A type of divination or fortune telling that uses features of the landscape. *The writers of the dictionary definition incorrectly assume that the "features" (forms) of the landscape are somehow "read," giving the geomancer a message.*

True geomancy is the art of using one's mind to "tune in" to the energy information matrix of the planet, thus obtaining information and guidance directly from Spirit. Those who wish to perform geomantic rituals seek out Power Spots for an obvious reason: The energy of the Earth is stronger at these places, thus making it easier to "tune in."

Geomancy is not only a type of "fortune telling" (becoming aware of energy as information) geomancy is also a holistic philosophy for understanding the Earth, and Mankind's place upon it. Geomantic philosophy assures us that we are one with the Earth, and that the energy of the Earth is the very force from which we draw our lives.

The art of geomancy includes the performance of rituals and meditations which help the people of the Earth to communicate with their planet. Group rituals are considered to be very important for maintaining planetary stability. The rituals of the modern Christian church began as pagan geomantic ritual....

Those who study geomancy find that many Christian churches in Europe are built upon Power Spots originally identified by pagan geomancers. It is interesting to note that the word pagan originally meant that a person was a country dweller, or of the Earth.

Sedona is in no way unique as a place where Human beings have identified a special power or presence in the natural features of the land. Since ancient times, those who are sensitive to the Spirit of nature have identified Power Spots such as Sedona, making them shrines or using them to conduct ceremonies which put them in touch with the Great Spirit and the Spirit of the Earth.

Power Spots in Europe that many of our ancestors worked with were used as sites to practice a form of Earth worship very similar to that of the Native American Medicine Wheel. These ceremonies were done in a circle in which the four directions were always honored, and marked with a cross...

The cross is the symbol of the union of cosmic forces, the coming together of the polarities which create the world. A cross may be defined as a Vortex: The intersection of angles. In the practice of geomancy a cross is used to mark a place where the strands of the Web of Life join together, thus forming a Power Spot.

All life and matter within our planet's gravity field are connected together with an energy matrix. Native American mystics speak of this as the "Web of Life"....The Web is multidimensional. It is a form of Spirit, intelligent energy. The Web is associated with our planet's gravitational and electromagnetic fields. The Sedona Vortices are just a few of the major Power Spots of our planet which are connected together in this Web of Life. Strands of the Web also travel through space connecting all things in the Universe.

The art of geomancy is directly concerned with working with the energies of the Web. Upon our Earthly plane most people can best understand the Web by thinking of it as Earth energy; the biomagnetic field of the Earth.

The wave pattern of our planet's biomagnetic field forms the strands of the Web. These strands are known to English-speaking Geomancers as ley lines. These natural lines of force connect all Power Spots and Vortices. Some modern geomancers refer to the Web as the "planetary grid."

The Web acts as a group mind for the inhabitants of the planet. It is a channel for information between minds. This is why we find Power Spots to make our special prayers. Our prayers are amplified and projected out to all other beings.

Spirit is intelligent Power - Energy is information.

Geomancers also speak of another type of Earth energy that behaves in a somewhat more mysterious and less predictable fashion than the ley lines. These flows of energy are known to us in the West by the Chinese words "feng shui." Seemingly controlled by a primal intelligence, this energy is said to be the Spirit of the Earth.

In China, the art of geomancy is referred to as feng shui. The words feng shui are Chinese for "wind and water," meaning these energies are as incomprehensible as the wind, and ungraspable as the water.

Feng shui forces are recognized by Chinese geomancers as a type of Chi (Life Force). While it may be impossible to explain the feng shui currents in a logical manner, many geomancers and students of feng shui believe that many (not all) currents of Life Force energy that travel along the Earth's surface follow the path of water as it flows beneath the surface of the Earth. Water is the lifeblood of our planet. Where water flows, life goes. This is true in both practical and metaphysical terms.

In the Sedona area the Web of Life which is woven around the Vortices is complemented by a generous flow of Chi (Life Force), which is carried through the Red Rock Country by underground rivers and streams.

It is my theory that certain types of Life Force energy are generated, and carried by water as it flows through the Earth's magnetic field. Our blood also interacts with the natural electromagnetic field of the Earth, generating Life Force energy within the body on the cellular level.

(This energy transfer is the result of the interaction of the same forces which are commonly used to generate electrical energy.)

Traditionally, dowsing rods* have been used to identify ley lines and flows of Earth energy such as the feng shui. But it is not usually necessary to have a dowsing rod to find a Power Spot. People who are in touch with the Earth are usually open enough to be able to find Power Spots with their intuition. In fact, people are drawn to some Power Spots like magnets....

Circles of stone such as this are truly one of the Mysteries of Sedona. Most locals know that to build a Wheel such as this is "against Forest service rules." This leads us to the conclusion that the rocks on the Medicine Wheel must move into place by themselves. As further evidence of this, Forest Service officials have noted that in some cases Wheels that have been dis-assembled by Forest Service workers have re-appeared "overnight."

*The use of dowsing rods is explained later in this book, in the section titled "Encountering the Forces of the Higher Planes." This particular section being one of the most important parts of this book, because it deals with invoking the Power of the Will.

THE EVOLUTION OF PLANETARY CONSCIOUSNESS
JOSE ARGUELLES, AND THE MAYAN FACTOR

Some of the material in this book was inspired by the work of Mr. Jose Arguelles.

Mr. Arguelles has some very interesting things to say about Mankind's role here on the planet Earth and our place in the cosmos. Particularly interesting are Mr. Arguelles ideas on: Resonance with energy/energy as information, the evolution of Human consciousness, and the understanding that we are the operators of the planet Earth.

If it were not for Mr. Arguelles many of us would be unaware of the Mayan Factor. Like the plot of a good science fiction story, our society is discovering that the Mayans, a group of people which some scholars consider to be almost stone age, were masters of a technology far more advanced than our own; the technology of pure thought... Will, and the direct contact with Spirit.

Much of the information which Mr. Arguelles has brought forth is based upon the Mayan calendar, an advanced numerical system that calibrates Earth time to the emanations from the infinite source of creation. An instrument which allows Human Beings on this planet to work with Galactic synchronization, therefore finding harmony with the Universal forces.

By comparing the dates of historical events and noting the periods when various trends, revolutions, and eras have come and gone, Mr. Arguelles is able to demonstrate that the Mayan system also charts the history of the Human Race.

Vortex explorers, and others who consider themselves to be on the cutting edge of Human evolution should find it particularly interesting that the Mayan Calendar indicates that the period of time which we are going through is a time of awakening planetary consciousness, and a passing away of social systems which inhibit societies growth.

At this time planetary evolution is being accelerated. All systems are speeding up and the room for error is diminishing, as the stakes for individual and planetary survival are getting higher. Those who are not open to new information will fall to the wayside.

We are once again beginning to understand our spiritual natures as children of the Earth, remembering that our entire planet is an energy field, in which all life, and all matter take part.

From my vantage point in Sedona, I can see that the Vortex phenomenon is merely a catalyst that has begun a process leading to world wide geomantic Earth healing ceremonies, which will bind the Human race together in love.

This is why I have found it important to include the Medicine Wheel Guide as part of this book. By using geomantic ceremonies to combine the energies of good people around the planet, we can develop enough power to heal all the warheads all the greedheads, and all the powerheads combined.

When thinking of these things I am reminded of Arthur C. Clarke's Science fiction book; *Childhood's End*. And I remind you that science fiction can be defined as future memory.

CHILDHOOD'S END

⊕ ABOUT SHAMANISM ⊕

It is important to remember that not all Shamanic techniques raise the consciousness or evolve the Human Spirit in a desirable manner. Like all magical practices there is a path of light and a path of darkness... a path of evolution, and a path of devolution... and both paths can appear very similar to the novice... So keep it light.

Many of the beliefs, meditations, and exercises, detailed in this book, can be regarded as forms of Shamanism...True Shamanism is the mystical experience of the Earth Spirit.

However, it is important to note that merely working with Earth Energy, or carrying a few crystals and feathers around does not make one a Shaman. The Shamanic path is not as glamorous or fun as certain writers who have recently popularized this term would have us think. Those who understand that facts of Shamanism know that to be a true Shaman with "magical powers" is not an easy path. One must undergo trials, and rigors...No one chooses to be a Shaman; they are chosen "by Spirit."

Like all mystical traditions, Shamanism requires that the student devote a great deal of time meditating and purifying themselves so that they can become a "clear channel" for the light. This means that if you do not spend a lot of time meditating, working with crystals, and otherwise improving yourself, how can you expect to be a Shaman? (Or any other sort of true mystic.)

The average Vortex explorer who reads this book should be content with simply trying to have an adventure, expand their consciousness, and re-establish their mystical bond with the Earth. Yes, it is common for Vortex energy to trigger paranormal experiences, but experiencing past lives, mental telepathy, or inter-dimensional communication with "space beings" does not make one a Shaman, however, any of these experiences would be a step in the right direction....

Carlos Castaneda's books contain valuable information about the mysterious possibilities and psychology of Shamanic training. These teachings can also help us understand the Vortex phenomenon. If you are drawn to Mr. Castaneda's work, and you feel that you understand it, then you have already begun your journey to the enchanted land.

Mr. Castaneda was a student of a Yaqui Indian "man of knowledge," whom we know as Don Juan Mateus. Don Juan traced his magical heritage to the Toltecs of Central America...The Toltecs are considered by many to be the heirs of the Mayan tradition....

Don Juan told Carlos that Spirit had chosen him to bring the secret teachings forward so that more Human Beings would have the chance to escape the cycle of life and death, thus becoming beings of pure Spirit.

And while Don Juan's path is not the only way, it remains the best publicized path of interdimensional initiation, opening many people's minds to possibilities they had not imagined existed.

Like all schools of mystery, the path that Don Juan followed was based on the belief that the world is an illusion which forms itself to fit the beliefs and expecta-tions of the observer. So it is perfectly fitting that this school of mystery was handed down from the Mayans themselves, who were, and are, masters of time-space illusion...(Read the first chapter of the Mayan Factor by Jose Arguelles....)

NEUROSHAMANISM

Only certain types of people become interested in the Vortices or metaphysics. They do so because they are ready to accept new information which will help them release the thought patterns of ordinary three dimensional reality as it is interpreted by the current group social consciousness.

(Everyone who isn't ready just stopped reading.) Now that I am amongst like minded friends I can speak my heart: Vortex energy works upon Humans on many different levels. One of the most interesting things that Vortex energy can do is to activate neural pathways which allow us to experience psychic awareness.

Activating these pathways can be compared to loading programs into a computer; it is a type of rapid learning. It is also a de-programming, a letting go of limited thought patterns.

The Vortex experience is a learning process which helps us understand new ways of perceiving reality and working with our environment. It is this sort of training which all schools of mysticism use: A de-programming of conditioned response, and an acceptance of new ideas which are taught by the direct experience of Spirit.

The most important part of Carlos Castaneda's training was the activation of unused portions of Carlos' awareness... The activation of neural pathways which control psychic awareness and the ability to work with the forces of pure Spirit. And the unlearning of conditioned responses which keep human beings well grounded in ordinary reality.

And so it is in honor of the evolutionary agents Juan, Carlos, Jose, Anton, and Tim that I have adopted the phrase Vortex Neuroshamanism to describe the art and practice of expanding the consciousness with Vortex energy.

WHAT IS A VORTEX?

Munds Mountain as seen from Uptown Sedona — Schnebly Hill Road travels through the Canyon at the base of this mountain.

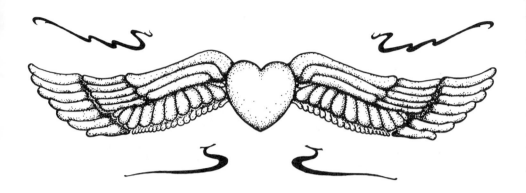

This rock spire is just below the Kachina Woman in Boynton Canyon.

⊕ WHAT IS A VORTEX? ⊕

Simply stated the Sedona Vortices are places where the natural electro-magnetic field of the Earth is strong.

It shall take many pages to explore the myths, theories, and facts of Vortex phenomenon; we begin now with simple explanations. This opening statement about the Vortices is followed by several pages which explore important ideas about Vortex energy and how the energy of the Vortices effects our minds and bodies. Feel free to skip ahead to the section that describes the Vortices themselves, but remember: in order to truly understand the Vortices, you shall have to read the entire book.

The geology of the Sedona area has produced rock formations that act as focal points for electromagnetic Earth energies, these focal points are what we call Vortices.

All Vortices are "electromagnetic." Individual Vortices usually having a dominant force, of either "electric" or "magnetic" energy. [Which is always accompanied by a trace of its complimentary force.]

This means that both types of Vortices share many common qualities. Their energies affect both our physical and spiritual bodies; expanding the consciousness, and healing the body.

Bell Rock and the Airport Vortex are electric Vortices. Cathedral Rock is a magnetic Vortex. Boynton Canyon contains both electric and magnetic Vortices.

ELECTRICAL VORTICES

Electric Vortices are good places for beginners to go, to "get the feel." They are excellent places for work on the higher mental planes through meditation and for projecting thoughts and prayers. Electric Vortices are places where the Earth releases electrical energy; they are energizing. The energy boost of these Vortices works directly upon the body, and indirectly upon our minds. As we increase the electrical energy within our body, circuits open up within our Central Nervous System which allow us to experience "new" levels of awareness: Our psychic abilities become awakened.

Small amounts of electrical energy are released into the atmosphere at the Earth's surface, this is known as the "corona discharge effect." The corona discharge along high points of the Earth's surface is greater than that of level ground. The sandstone spires in the Sedona area are ideal discharge points for electrical energy from the Earth.

Some of this electrical energy is absorbed by the air, thus forming "negative ions". These ions energize the body as we breathe them in. Electrical Vortex energy is also a form of Spirit - intelligent energy - a connection with the creative forces of the Universe....

Electrical terms carry no moral judgments: Electrons carry a negative charge which energizes, and protons carry a positive charge which binds.

Magnetic Vortices are perhaps even more mysterious than Electrical Vortices. They exist as energy fields which have no physical substance. The energies of Magnetic Vortices are closely associated with the etheric (non-physical) level of existence.

The energies of the Magnetic Vortices are subtle, having more effect upon the Spirit level of existence and the inner levels of the mind than upon the physical body. Magnetic Vortices are excellent places for deep meditation, accessing inner levels of knowledge, and contacting the "Spirit of the Earth." This type of Vortex is also noted for its ability to trigger past life recall and other types of paranormal experience such as telepathic communication with spirit guides.

Magnetic Vortices have the ability to re-align the energy field of the Human body. Or in simpler words: Magnetic Vortices "tune up" the Aura so that it resonates properly with the energies of the Earth. The subtle electrical energy current produced by a Magnetic Vortex also helps to rejuvenate the physical body on the cellular level.

Magnetic Vortices occur where there are "veins" of iron bearing basalt (ancient lava deposits) running through sandstone formations. These "basalt intrusions" are conductors of electromagnetic energies from deep in the Earth, and a field (or Vortex) is produced around them.

Cathedral Rock is the strongest Magnetic Vortex in the Sedona area. There are many other "minor" Magnetic Vortices scattered throughout the area, which are often marked by veins of crumbling dark grey rocks (basalt intrusions).

Magnetic Vortices are sometimes naively referred to as negative. This does not mean they are bad; what is meant is that the energy tends to have a receiving, or an attracting nature.

The Vortex at Cathedral Rock does not rob power from people. It cycles energy through our bodies, cleansing, energizing, and balancing our personal energy field.

The magnetic energy of Boynton Canyon emanates from many basalt intrusions in the mountains which form the canyon.

The Electrical Vortex in Boynton Canyon is near the entrance to the canyon, and very close to the parking lot.

Please read the section of this book which is about Boynton Canyon, before you visit this place.

The most enduring myth of the Red Rock Country concerns the "Spirit" of Boynton Canyon. It is an undeniable fact that Boynton Canyon is a place of mysterious power.

Many Indian legends have not survived the test of time, but the legend of the Goddess in Boynton Canyon has persisted. The Yavapai Indians who lived in the Red Rock Country before the arrival of the White Man, considered Boynton Canyon to be a sacred place. Indian legend tells us that there is an Earth Goddess that "lives" in Boynton Canyon.

The legend of the Goddess in Boynton Canyon is particularly intriguing to those who believe that the shift towards planetary awareness and global healing is dependent upon humanity's becoming aware of the feminine Spirit of the Earth.

Key ideas which lead to an understanding of the Vortex phenomenon

1. Everything within our planetary sphere is part of a common field of energy which links all things together. The Human mind, body, and spirit share a common resonance with the planetary energy field.

2. The major portion of our planet's energy field is produced by three key elements which also make up most of our planet's mass; iron, silicon, and oxygen. This planet's magnetic field is produced by iron, much of which is in the form of iron oxide. The subtle planetary energy field of Spirit is held in focus by silicon oxide, which is otherwise known as quartz. (Spirit = intelligent energy.)

3. It is these three elements which make up much of the red rock formations in Sedona... Our bodies' energy field has a natural resonance with the elements which make up the red rocks.

4. Science tells us that our bloodstream carries many magnetized particles of iron oxide (magnetite). The membrane which is in front of our "Third Eye" (the pituitary gland, our organ of psychic awareness) also contains magnetite crystals. Given these facts, we should begin to see that there is a common resonance between these elements in our blood, our brains, and the red rocks themselves.

⊕ FROM WHENCE THE VORTEX COMES ⊕

This is perhaps the most important page in this entire book. Study this page, and spend time thinking about what these words mean.

When we speak of a Vortex of Earth energy being either electrical or magnetic, we are not only referring to the presence of electromagnetic energy; we are also speaking of a place where the very fabric of the Universe is distorted in a manner that allows power from the dimension of pure energy to "leak through" into our dimension.

The words electricity and magnetism help our logical minds begin to grasp the forces of universal creation which create our world. We are, however, missing the point if we always insist on describing the forces we encounter at the Vortices with the terms we use to describe ordinary reality.

True mystics know that the only way to truly understand the energies of Spirit is to go beyond definitions. We must use our powers of meditation to help us see beyond the veil and experience Spirit directly.

Many people who work with the Vortices believe that the strongest component of the Vortex exists not on the physical plane but on the astral and etheric planes. Anything we detect as being either electric or magnetic is actually a secondary effect of a much more profound force that exists in the realm of Spirit.

A Vortex is a place where the energies of the Spiritual realm are entering the physical. When we "tune in" to the energy of a Vortex our mind and body are able to learn of Spirit directly from Spirit: Energy is information (Jose Arguelles).

Simply meditating, anywhere, wherever you are, also helps you learn directly from Spirit. Remember that Spirit is the force from which our world is woven, it is with us at all times. When we quiet our minds and "go within" we learn the lessons of Spirit.

THE SYMBOL OF INTERDIMENSIONAL REALITY

Since ancient times we have used symbols to help our logical minds grasp metaphysical truths that are beyond the limits of ordinary reality. It is from the Ancients we get this symbol, and the teaching that our world coincides with another realm; the realm of pure Spirit.

The two interlocking circles represent the world of Spirit and the world of physical reality. The center part of this glyph represents the "crack between the worlds," the Vortex through which energy flows between the two realms.

This overlapping of the worlds is happening on many levels, and it is in fact impossible for our three-dimensional minds to fully comprehend how these things work. True understanding comes through the experiences gained by meditation, and the direct experience of Spirit which meditation brings.

The Truth is beyond words.

Scientists tell us that the entire Universe is a unified field of energy; every square inch of space - even the pure vacuum of deep space is full of energy. Magnetism is a secondary effect of this field of pure energy as it interacts with matter. Magnetic energy has no substance; it exists as a non-physical "field"....

For many years scientists believed that there was an element, or dimension through which energies such as light, and radio waves traveled in, or *originated from.* This dimension was referred to as "aether," or "ether." The concept of ether was "borrowed" from the ancient schools of the mysteries by renaissance scientists who based their scientific theories upon a mystical view of the Universe.

Theories based upon the existence of ether were popular among scientists until the 1920s. Modern physicists no longer base their theories upon the existence of ether; instead they prefer to say that there are at least ten dimensions parallel to our own....

A student of metaphysics may casually refer to the dimensions of pure energy as "ether." The phrase "etheric plane" is often used as a generic term to describe the entire spectrum of "energy realms" (dimensions) which co-exist side by side with our own three dimensional time-space reality. Often we refer to things (such as the Human Aura) as being on the "etheric plane."

As metaphysicians, we know that magnetic fields and electrical energy are manifestations of pure Life Force on the physical plane, and that the electromagnetic phenomenon of the physical plane draws its energy from the Universal source that exists in the non-physical "ether" (the realm of Spirit).

Iron produces magnetic fields of seemingly limitless duration because it is capable of tapping in to the Universal field of energy (which exists on the "etheric plane" "side by side" with our own reality), and changing that energy into a magnetic field. (This is known as transduction. Quartz crystals are also energy transducers.)

⊕ THERE IS ELECTRICITY IN THE AIR ⊕

Vortex energy is sometimes referred to as "psychic energy." This is because we know that the electromagnetic Earth energy of the Vortices is capable of stimulating our minds in a manner that triggers "psychic phenomena" i.e. events which can be considered to be "paranormal" (beyond the "normal" experience of life).

The electromagnetic field of our planet works upon our minds in at least two ways: First, if our bodies are able to absorb the proper amount of electrons (usually in the form of negative oxygen ions in the air), our "electronic matrix" will be fully charged. At this time our central nervous system will be operating at peak efficiency, and our glands will be producing the hormones which are associated with optimum health: We become "well tuned."

(The rock spires around Sedona "give off" electrical charges which produce negative oxygen ions.)

Secondly, the Human body is "tuned" to the electromagnetic field of the Earth. When we allow ourselves to relax, our minds automatically "tune in" to what is known as the "Earth wave."

It is a scientific fact that the stability of our bodily functions is dependent upon the electronic stimulation of our planet's electromagnetic field. This was proven by NASA scientists in the mid-sixties.

The first Astronauts to go into orbit became mysteriously ill, but soon recovered upon returning to Earth. NASA scientists speculated that the astronauts had become ill because they had been deprived the stimulation of the Earth's electromagnetic field.

This was later proven when the Astronauts metabolism remained stable after a low power transmitter was placed in the space capsule to create an artificial electromagnetic field that pulsed at 7.83 cycles per second.

NASA scientists named the wave that occurs between 7-8 cps: the Earth Wave. Please note that the Alpha brain wave state, which is associated with relaxation, meditation, psychic, and paranormal phenomenon also occurs between 7-8 cps... Therefore, when we relax, and meditate, we are resonating with the Earth Wave.

Before negative ions or Earth Waves were ever heard of, those who wanted to develop their mental abilities were encouraged to do things that naturally increase the bodies' electrical potential.

Students on the spiritual path are always encouraged to do breathing exercises. These exercises allow the body to absorb increased amounts of electrical energy from the air. They also help the body balance and circulate its energy.

Those who want to experience higher levels of consciousness are also encouraged to drink pure water, and eat live healthy foods which are known to be "full of Life Force." Live foods carry desirable electrical energy to the body. Processed foods, carbonated beverages and beer, rob the body of electrical energy.

The true Vortex experience is obtained by those who take care of their body. The "psychic energy" of the Vortices is electrical energy; when our bodies' full electrical potential is reached our mental abilities are increased.

⊕ THE TRANSITION ZONE ⊕

The geology of the Sedona area is noted for its rock formations, which act as "focal points" for electromagnetic Earth energies. These "focal points" are what we call Vortices.

According to geologists, Sedona is in the transition zone between the Desert Basin and the Colorado Plateau. The transition zone is a large region that runs East to West, across the state of Arizona and on into New Mexico. In some areas it is up to fifty miles wide. Sedona is at the northern limit of the transition zone, at the base of the Colorado plateau.

Oak Creek Fault runs right through the Sedona area at a right angle to the transition zone. This fault is a forty-mile-long "crack" on the stable land mass of the Colorado Plateau. It is considered to be a minor fault, and very much unlike the huge splits in the Earth which are characteristic of active earthquake faults... (so don't worry.)

The Vortex activity in the Sedona area seems to indicate that Oak Creek Fault allows an abnormal amount of electromagnetic Earth Energy to emerge from deep in the Earth.

This energy is conducted by iron-bearing veins of basalt (lava), which were formed long ago during an age of volcanic activity....

Oak Creek Fault gave birth to the most powerful mountains in Arizona - the San Francisco Peaks. These ancient volcanoes are located at the north end of the Oak Creek fault, some thirty miles north of Sedona near Flagstaff.

The geology of the Sedona is noted for its rock formations that act as "focal points" for electromagnetic Earth energies. These focal points are what we call Vortices.

The sandstone formations in the Sedona area contain a great deal iron oxide (which gives them their red color), and silicon in the form of finely ground quartz. Silicon is well known for its electronic qualities, and quartz, for its ability to enhance the energy field known as the Human Aura....

Geologists tell us that the foundation upon which the sandstone formations of Sedona stand is composed primarily of iron. An electrically conductive and magnetic element, iron, is an energy transducer; it produces magnetic fields by "tapping in" to the unified field of energy that exists throughout the Universe... Every magnet is a "Vortex" of magnetic energy... *The magnetic Vortices of Sedona are formed around iron bearing veins of basalt.*

With this information we should be able to easily understand that the sandstone formations of the Sedona Vortices have electronic characteristics. Storing and releasing electrical energy from the inner Earth, and acting as focal points for magnetic fields: Vortices.

⊕ CRYSTALS ⊕

Those who are interested in developing their psychic abilities can accelerate their learning by working with quartz crystals. Many people who take the time to learn how to use these crystals often find that knowledge comes to them directly from the "higher planes."

Just as our physical bodies are "tuned" to the electromagnetic field of the Earth, our Auras (our energy bodies) are tuned to the planetary energy field which is focused by the quartz crystals that form much of our planet.

Opening up to the energies of quartz crystals activates "circuitry" within our Central Nervous System that helps us become more aware of the energy field of our planet. However, merely wearing a quartz crystal will not have a noticeable affect upon the consciousness. A crystal has to be worked with in order for it to become "activated."

Wearing a crystal helps to develop an energy bond between the crystal, the person who is wearing it, and the Earth. But in order for the wearer to actually work the crystal, it should be held in the hands during meditation, or it should be gazed at. Mental commands should be directed towards the crystal, asking it to wake up and do its work. A crystal can be asked to perform a function, such as protection, or it can be "listened to" for guidance.

Perhaps the quickest way to learn how to work with a crystal is to place it in the center of your forehead and then focus upon that spot. When you first begin to do this, do it for only a short while or else you might overload your circuitry.

Generally speaking, the best place to wear a crystal is over your Solar Plexus. (The group of muscles and nerves located at the front of the body at the base of the rib cage where the ribs join in the middle.) Yogis, mystics, and Native American shaman refer to this spot as the center of the physical and the Spiritual bodies. The solar plexus is one of our bodies' seven energy centers (chakras). It is sometimes referred to as the "seat of the Will."

It is easy to wear a crystal over this spot; simply find a crystal pouch or a piece of jewelry that hangs low....

Quartz crystals are formed within the Earth by superheated water. This water comes from deep within the Earth, who knows what subtle spiritual energies this water carries? Perhaps one of the reasons that the vibrations of Humans and quartz complement each other so well is that these crystals have absorbed some of the spiritual essence of the planet itself.

Due to the volcanic activity in the Sedona area it is entirely possible that there may be deposits of various types of crystals throughout the Red Rock Country. The mysterious energies we encounter throughout this area may be energy fields produced by crystals... Whatever the case, we know for a fact that Sedona's sandstone formations contain countless tiny quartz crystals, otherwise known as sand...

ENCOUNTERING THE FORCES
OF THE "HIGHER PLANES"

WHAT IS A DOWSING ROD? AND HOW DOES A DOWSING ROD WORK?

Human Beings have the ability to work with a wide spectrum of "cosmic energies" that go virtually unnoticed to most beings of the physical plane. Vortex energy is one of these energies. It is truly a cosmic energy which is not limited to the planet Earth - it is part of the Unified Field of energy which forms the Universe itself.

The energy of the Vortices is hard to define. We often refer to it as being electromagnetic, but it is important to understand that there are other forces involved that do not fit neatly into the definitions of electromagnetism.

We need to become aware of the fact that there is an entire spectrum of cosmic forces from which all things draw power. Of particular interest are those forces which affect the Human mind and body directly, and that can be controlled by the proper use of Will - The Forces of Life.

Dowsing rods, pendulums, and crystals help us become aware of our abilities to work with the energies of the higher planes. While we work with these tools, we are encouraging Life Force and other cosmic energies to flow through our system, thereby activating dormant abilities and accelerating our spiritual growth.

Some very interesting experiments and demonstrations can be performed with dowsing rods, pendulums, and crystals which seem to prove the existence of these energies, and the fact that Human beings are capable of controlling them.

The use of Will is an important key to the successful use of these tools. Metaphysical students know that Will is a powerful spiritual force which in many ways defies logical explanation. Will can often be better understood by observing its results, rather than trying to analyze the way it works.

Operators of dowsing rods, pendulums, and crystals control their tools by giving them mental commands. In this case, Will, can be defined as the energy created by a mental command... Simply giving a mental command for something to happen invokes the Will to produce results on the spiritual and physical planes.

⊕ ⊕ ⊕

When the operator of a dowsing rod or pendulum is attempting to detect something, they hold the mental image of that thing in their minds while they focus upon their instrument.

Experienced operators learn how to interpret the movements of their tool, revealing the presence of physical objects and energy fields, or to bring forth knowledge from their higher selves.

Perhaps the most mysterious thing about these tools is the fact that they can be made to move without any physical encouragement. The Operator of a dowsing rod or a pendulum can hold their hand absolutely still and their instrument may still move. This seems to imply that Human Beings can cause physical objects to move with the power of their minds!

This brings forth an interesting question: Since most people are capable of successfully operating these devices (making them move through an act of Will), can they cause other physical objects to move?*

⊕ ⊕ ⊕

The action of the dowsing rod and pendulum defies logical explanation. At this point we can only speculate on the hows, and the whys of their operation.

Many modern dowsers believe that most things, be they material objects or sources of pure energy, have a "field" that can somehow be detected by the Operators and translated into movement of their tools. There is no scientific way to prove the existence of these fields. However, the concept of field has proved to be a useful theory that helps our logical minds accept the physical evidence....

Since these fields are thought to be similar to radio waves, modern dowsers have adopted the terms "radionic energy" and "radionic fields" to describe them. The modern jargon describes the tools that are used to detect these energies as "radionic antenna."

Whether the radionic fields exist or not, cannot yet be proven. What can be said with certainty is that Human Beings do have the circuitry to work with many types of energies that exist on the higher realms, and that we can extend our capabilities to a point that defies logical explanation.

Radionic antenna are an extension of our bodies' natural senses. If we allow ourselves to accept the things that they show us, they prove that things such as the Human Aura and Life Force Energies do exist.

Understanding the theory, and operation of these tools can help students develop their psychic abilities and understand the Vortex phenomenon.

AUTHORS NOTE

Certain types of radionic energy can be scientifically detected with various types of exotic scientific equipment, including a device which is known as the "superconducting quantum interference device," otherwise known as SQUID... This device has been able to detect the Human Aura and its energy centers (chakras). The SQUID has also been able to detect the energy of ley lines. (The energies of the Human Aura and the Ley Lines qualify as Radionic Energies.) Unfortunately we are going to have to wait a few more years for this information to become mainstream: Certain powers within the establishment have a vested interest in suppressing valid scientific information about Spirit. If you are interested in perusing this subject; I recommend the out of print book: Brain, Body, and Electromagnetism, by John Evans.

---

* The answer is yes, Human Beings do have the ability to move physical objects with their minds. Uri Geller is perhaps the most famous example of this. Mr. Geller's ability to create magnetic fields and move physical objects without touching them was certified by a group of scientists at the Stanford research center. (Legend has it that Mr. Geller has had success using a pendulum and a map to locate precious metals and strategic minerals, and is now quite wealthy...)

⊕ CONTROLLING THE WILL ⊕

The ability to control Life Force Energies by an act of Will is a natural Human ability....

My friend and associate, Mr. John Armbruster, gives lectures on the Human Aura. In one part of his lecture he uses a dowsing rod to measure the strength of one of the participant's Aura.

Many of the people with whom he has chosen to do this experiment have very little practical metaphysical knowledge or training, but this experiment proves time and time again that each person has the intuitive ability to control these energies by an act of Will....

When the volunteer first stands up, the emanations of their Aura are usually quite strong and can be easily detected with a dowsing rod up to approximately six feet away from the volunteer.

After demonstrating to the audience that the dowsing rod appears to be reacting to the volunteer's Aura, John then tells the volunteer to "draw their Aura in"....

The volunteer is told to give themselves the mental command to "draw their Aura in". While this is being done, John cannot detect the volunteer's Aura unless he holds the "Rod" near an energy center (chakra) on the volunteer's body. *The volunteer's Aura no longer extends several feet, but has been drawn in - close to their body.*

This demonstration appears to prove not only the existence of the Aura (as detected by the dowsing rod), but also that *untrained* people have the natural ability to control their Aura with an act of Will... Even though they have had no previous experience doing so.

⊕ ⊕ ⊕

Will cannot be understood with the terms that are usually used to define "normal reality." Will is the ability to command the forces of nature...Will in action often defies logical explanation.

All meditation practices train the mind to be able to concentrate, thereby giving the meditator the ability to "focus their intent." The ability to focus the intent is the key factor in the control of Will.

The more focused the mind is upon a particular goal, the more likely it is that the Will shall cause that thing to become realized.

The use of dowsing rods, pendulums, and crystals trains the mind to focus upon one thing, thus training the "intent"...which controls the Will.

These experiences also help the Operator become familiar with working with the "Forces of Life." As a person practices working with these metaphysical light energies, new circuits in the Operator's system are activated, leading to advanced states of awareness and paranormal abilities.

Light Meditations as described in other parts of this book are perhaps the best sort of training for working with these metaphysical energies.

Crystals are one of the easiest things for a beginner to "dowse," especially crystals that the beginner has worn, or worked with for some time. These crystals will usually have become adjusted to their owner's energy field, and there will be a sympathetic vibration between the two. (Friends are also good to practice on, the open palm of a good friend is usually easy to get a reading from.)

Beginners should sit in a relaxed position, perhaps with their legs crossed, resting their hands (which hold the rod) on their legs in a manner that steadies the rod so that body movements will not cause the tip of the rod to move very much.

I feel that it is particularly important for beginners to hold their rod in a relaxed, steady manner so that when their rod starts reacting to the energy of the crystal they will have no doubt that the movement of their rod is being caused by an energy field and mental concentration... not hand movements.

After the beginner has found a relaxed position, they should place their crystal in front of themselves, very close to the tip of their dowsing rod, and then concentrate upon the tip of their instrument while giving themselves the "mental command": I am going to pick up the energy field of this crystal, and my dowsing rod will move....

Many beginners find that when they concentrate on their dowsing rod as they hold it near their crystal, the rod starts to move right away. And like many other things they have learned, once they "get the feel," they are then able to explore the possibilities at will.... [If the rod does not begin to move right away, be patient and keep concentrating.]

Even though this technique works well with beginners, it can very rapidly turn into an advanced crystal meditation....

Dowsing a crystal sets up a strong energy bond between the Operator and the crystal, becoming a type of "closed loop." A deep meditive state can be reached this way which creates a strong psychic link between the crystal and the Operator. Once this "link" has been established the Operator can easily enter an altered state of consciousness from which a great deal of wisdom can be accessed.

This technique activates the crystal... After you have dowsed the crystal for approximately fifteen minutes, hold it up to your forehead in the "Third Eye" area and do breathing exercises, or light meditations. This will open the psychic channel through which you can contact your spirit guides and access information from the higher planes....

When the energies of the Operator and the crystal have become synchronized, it is the ideal time for the Operator to use their mental energy to program their crystal to perform various tasks for them, such as psychic protection and dream guidance.

THE HAND IS MORE SENSITIVE TO LIFE FORCE ENERGIES THAN ANY SORT OF DOWSING ROD

If you want to learn how to work with Earth energy you should practice using your body to help your mind merge with the vibrations of the Earth. Your hands and your feet are two of your most important contact points with the Earth. It is good to practice using your hands and feet as energy receptors...your body can teach you things which no one else can.

While you are walking, try rubbing your palms together while you practice taking correct breaths; as you do this, give yourself the "mental command" to absorb energy. You should find that your level of awareness is increased by doing this exercise, and that you may also feel that you have become energized....

This exercise is known to stimulate the hands, thus making them more sensitive to the natural energies which surround us. After you have walked for awhile, rubbing your hands together and absorbing energy, experiment using your hands to sense energy fields... If you learn to trust your inner feelings you should find that you can sense many types of energy with the palms of you hands.

When you come up on a place in the hills that you think might be a Power Spot, hold your hands out straight in front of yourself with the palms down, and ask yourself if you can feel the "pulse of the Earth"... Then try sensing the energy with your hands held palms up: Do you get a different feeling when you hold your hands palms up?

The hands can be used to draw energy into the body. There is no set position for the hands, however, when one wants to become a "Rainbow Bridge", and draw power into the Earth, the hands are usually left in their normal position at the sides.

At other times, particularly when you want to merge with the pulse of the Earth, the hands can be held straight in front of you, or straight out to the side with the palms either up or down.

Perhaps the most powerful hand position is over the head. After you have climbed the mountain, and meditated in other ways... hold your hands high over your head and give thanks to the Great Spirit!

The hands are also energy projectors. We have all heard of the "healing touch." This is the ability of the Human to channel Life Force into another person for healing purposes... All massage done with good intent transfers healing energy into the person being massaged. We may however increase the healing power of the massage by giving ourselves the "mental command" to project healing energy into the person being massaged.

THE DOWSING ROD

Dowsing rods and pendulums are the "tools" of the geomancer, the folk healer, and the fortune teller. These tools are used to help their "Operator" detect energy fields and to obtain guidance from their higher selves.

Traditional dowsing rods have been made of willow or fruitwood. Modern dowsers may also use "rods" constructed from many different and seemingly unlikely materials, such as metal and plastic.

Pendulums work on the same principle as the dowsing rod. However they are not well suited for outdoor work, being more of an instrument of meditation, useful for obtaining guidance from the higher self, and as a tool to diagnose physical ailments. Questions can be asked, and the movement of the pendulum can be used to interpret the answer.

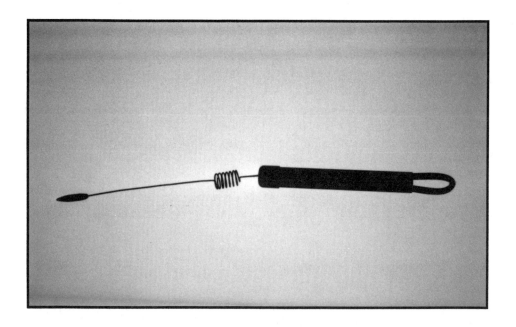

There are many types of radionic antenna that can be used for metaphysical work. The "rod" pictured here is similar to the famous Aura Meter (originally designed by Verne Cameron). Beginning dowsers often have good results with this type of rod.

I obtained this rod from my friend John Armbruster. The body is copper pipe, the "antenna" is brass rod. The antenna is attached to a loop of co-ax cable. (Which can be seen extending from the end of the tube which is opposite the antenna.)

If you feel that you would like learn more about dowsing, please write to me care of the Vortex Society.

THE LAND OF ENCHANTMENT, A COMMON SENSE GUIDE FOR VORTEX EXPLORERS

The two hills of Airport Vortex — the road is on the other side of these hills.

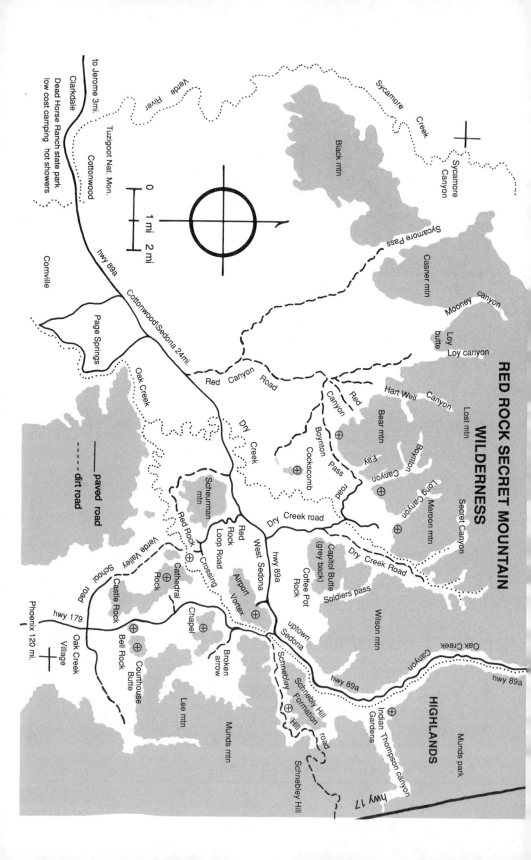

I encourage you to study the maps I am providing you with, so that you can begin to become acquainted with Sedona.

When you arrive in Sedona, check notices on the various bulletin boards at the crystal shops and book stores around town. Attending the events or ceremonies which are advertised upon these bulletin boards is an excellent way to get in contact with the locals.

When you get to Sedona you will want to drive around and look things over. But please remember that you cannot do everything in a couple of days. In fact, if you try to do too much, you may find that by the end of your stay you may have accomplished very little.

Those who rush around from place to place are missing the point entirely. After you have looked things over it is important to settle down and do one thing at a time. Remember that you came here seeking spiritual insight, so don't forget to spend time quietly meditating outside.

Plan to spend full days, or half days at one area. Bring some food, some water, and a working flashlight. (In case you get caught out after dark.) Always try to stick around and watch the sunset. You can usually get back to your car before it gets dark.

⊕ ⊕ ⊕

After you have become familiarized with the Sedona area, I suggest that you focus on getting in touch with just a few places that are special to you. So instead of running around wondering what to do, you always have special places that you are familiar with. Special places which you can return to time after time.

You can choose a quiet spot off the beaten trail where you can do some serious meditating. Or for fun, you could set up camp right beside a trail somewhere and talk to the people who come along. This can be quite entertaining, and you never know who you might meet.

⊕ ⊕ ⊕

Here in Sedona we hike all year around. It is never too hot or too cold for hardy individuals to venture out, and there are several months each year of moderate temperatures which everyone finds quite agreeable. But remember, midday Summer temperatures can easily reach one hundred degrees, so remember to wear a hat and some sunscreen and take plenty of water along. A wise adventurer may decide to explore during the mornings, the late afternoon and evenings, staying someplace cool during the hot part of the day.

During warm months I suggest that you get up early and hike in the mornings; The air and the light can be fantastic! If you work up a sweat in the afternoon, perhaps you might like to head for the creek for a swim. Afternoon naps by the creekside are proven methods of rejuvenation. *Do not drink creek water! too many people live along the creek, and the bacteria count can get rather high.* (Don't worry if you get a few drops in your mouth, it probably will not hurt you.)

Fall and Spring have both warm and cool days, but it is important to remember that a warm afternoon can give way to a rather cool evening, so be prepared! During the Fall and Spring it is a good idea to always set out on a hike with a sweater or light jacket in your daypack. Always carry water and something to snack on. (Dried fruit, such as figs or dates, make excellent trail food.)

Whatever season it is, during cloudy weather it is a good idea to stay of out narrow canyons and to keep to the high ground. Arizona is flash flood country. Rainstorms several miles away can send deadly walls of water down canyons and gullies. Some of the heaviest rainfalls occur in late July, August, and September, so watch it.

It is a good idea to check local conditions before going hiking or camping. A simple phone call to the Sedona ranger station is all it takes to find out about weather conditions, or fire restrictions.

Always avoid going to the bathroom near steams, springs, and wells. This is one of the reasons the water in Oak Creek is not safe to drink. Decomposing human waste creates bacteria that is deadly to Human Beings. Solid Human waste should always be buried about ten inches below the soil. If it is not, it becomes both a health hazard and a rather unsightly landmark.

Snakes hide out and hunt in the bushes. Knowing this fact should give you a good reason to stay on the trail. The other good reason for staying on the trail is that if you go off the trail you are probably damaging plants. The plants are living things and deserve respect. They also hold the soil, thus preventing erosion.

When many people visit the same area and they do not stay on the trails, the native plants get torn up. As you visit Power Spots such as Bell Rock and the Airport Vortices, notice how many plants have been damaged by careless hikers. The excessive damage to plants in these areas is simply pathetic.

It is especially important to stay on the trails in the spring time. This is the time when the grasses, and weeds are first sprouting and they are very tender. These small plants are very important. They prevent erosion. If they get stomped early in the spring, the patch of soil in which they were hoping to take root may get washed away.

People with dogs should take note: Dogs frequently turn out to be a real nuisance while on trips. Rattlesnakes are rough on dogs, and city dogs often run off after rabbits, or some other thing, and are hard to get back (if at all).

Rabbits, as well as all other rodents around here have disease carrying fleas. This is no joke. Often, the best thing to do is to leave Rover home.

NEVER HANDLE ANY RODENTS (especially wild rabbits).

RATTLESNAKES AND COMMON SENSE ABOUT OUTDOOR ADVENTURES

Here in Sedona we see so few snakes, many people tend to forget that they are here.

Snakes tend to avoid places where they encounter people. Popular Vortices and well used trails are usually snake free. Isolated areas such as the back of Long Canyon, are places where you had better be careful.

The best way to avoid snake bite is to be aware of the times when they are out and to KEEP YOUR EYES OPEN! Look where you are walking! And stay on the trail at all times! Do not walk through bushes.

Warm summer nights are times when the snakes are out. (Keep your eyes, and your nose out for skunks too...) Use a flashlight to guide your steps, and try to avoid sleeping on the ground without a tent. Snakes are heat seekers and they have been known to follow people into their sleeping bags. You should also be aware of the fact that scorpions have this same nasty habit of cuddling up with people at night, they also like to hide in shoes and boots. So always shake out your shoes and your clothes before you put them on. [Scorpion bites are very seldom deadly.]

Day or night, you will never encounter a snake if it is cold. Snakes are cold blooded and they hibernate when it is cold.

During fall and spring on warm afternoons you might encounter snakes sunning themselves on rocks.

Doctors advise those who are bitten by a snake to leave the wound alone and seek medical attention. **Remain as calm as possible;** snakebite victims have been known to become badly overexcited, thus making matters much worse... Anti-venom is supposedly effective for up to three hours after a bite: However, no one is going to waste any time getting to a hospital.

If someone gets bit by a snake, try to capture it, or at least try to remember what it looks like. This information is helpful in finding the right anti-venom. Don't panic. Find a phone, dial 911, and ask which clinic to go to. At the time of this writing, there is an emergency medical clinic in Sedona, but the only hospital in this area is in Cottonwood, which is about twenty miles west of Sedona.

THREE SNAKEBITE FACTS:

One: Twenty five percent of all known "single strike" snakebites are "dry"... no venom is injected. (But don't let 'em bite twice.)

Two: A dead snake can still bite. (yuck!)

Three: Only two people have been known to die from snakebite in Arizona since 1962.

A friend of mine who used to work for a tour company told me that I shouldn't even mention snakes, because it scares people. He said that in all the time he had been in Sedona, he had never seen a rattlesnake, so why should I scare people with snake stories? The answer to this is simple: Don't be frightened, be aware.

The reader of these words will probably never encounter a snake in Sedona. This is particularly true if they only visit popular areas.

Trails lead to all the good places. If you do not know where to go, all you have to do is follow the trail.

The best way to find the trail is to start from the place where people usually park their cars. Look down at the ground, if there is a trail there you will be able to see a ribbon of bare earth leading in between the bushes. Usually, there will also be footprints.

Sometimes when you get to a place where the trail "branches off", or is indistinct, the best route will often be marked with a small pile of stones. These small piles are placed there by people who want to help you find the way, so keep your eyes open for little piles of stone or ribbons tied into tree branches.

Typically, if you miss the trail you will end up walking for a little way only to find that the brush is getting thicker and thicker. You will either have to go crashing through the brush to get back on the right trail, or you will have to backtrack.

Crashing through the brush is a not a good practice. You can get scratched up or tear your clothes, and it is also hard on the bushes.

Every time a person goes crashing through the bushes they break off some branches. Trees and bushes around here grow slowly, so every little twig or branch counts. Damage to the forest is cumulative, over the period of years things can really get torn up.

Snakes can also be encountered while you are crashing through the bushes. So please stay on the trail.

Pay careful attention to your footing while you are on steep trails and mountain sides. Keep your hands out of your pockets, and your eyes upon the trail!

I never could understand how anyone could get lost in a narrow canyon. Let's face it, there are only two ways you can go; up or down.

If you ever get confused, stop, and think for a moment. In a canyon, you can either go up (in) or down (out). Look at your surroundings. You should be able to tell which way the ground is sloping. Usually, while in the Sedona area, as we leave our cars and go into the canyons, we are going up. So if we want to get back to our cars we should go down. Right?

You can also look for "landmarks." These are things such as trees, rocks, and mountains that we remember seeing on the trail or in the distance.

As you go along make mental notes of landmarks which catch your eye, such as: "We turned when we got to this burned tree." Or you might take note of a mountain in the distance, and later in the day, as you make your way back to your car, you might think: "That mountain was behind me as I walked off from my car, so now I should walk towards that mountain to find my car."

⊕ FIRES ⊕

The desert grasslands of Sedona are often quite dry. Please be very careful with your fires, and please respect seasonal fire restrictions.

I seldom build a fire when I camp. I find that if I have a fire, I tend to stare at it. Not only is this bad for the eyes, it keeps the happy camper from really experiencing what the night is really like. Oh yes, you might look at the stars for a few minutes, but you will always end up staring at the fire.

To cook only takes a very small fire, a so called "pocket fire." A fire like this can be made very quickly and easily from small twigs gathered from the ground near your camp. With a small fire it is easy to do things such as boil water and pop corn, because you can easily control the heat.

I find that two or three head sized (or smaller) rocks, with the fire in between works well for most cooking. You can put your pot on top of the crack between the rocks and feed the twigs in from the side. These sort of fires are also easy to put out, therefore, they are less of a fire hazard.

A FIRE PERMIT IS REQUIRED

Obtain fire permits at the Ranger station. At the time of this writing, the Sedona Ranger station is near the Crystal Castle, on Brewer road. Within two years there should be a new Ranger station on highway 179 near the Chapel of the Holy Cross.

Always build your fire away from brush, and never under or near a tree. Remember that wind can carry sparks many feet into dry brush, and that large fires can reach out, or up to set nearby trees on fire. Roots in the ground below fires can also be fire hazards. They can be caught on fire and slowly "burn back" into a dead tree, starting a fire long after the campers are gone.

If you must have a fire it is a good idea to bring your own wood. Do not attack the trees! Remember that you are in the land of enchantment, and trees are often inhabited by Earth Spirits... I would like you to take special notice of the trees when you are out and about. Often times a gnarly tree marks a Power Spot.

On nights when there is little or no moonlight, the stars can look very intense, and after you have been in the full darkness for awhile, you should actually be able to see fairly well. In fact many people who have never really experienced the outdoors in the nighttime are amazed at how well they can see after their eyes become adjusted!

Whenever you go out at night it is of course always a good idea to have a good working flashlight. Small flashlights which fit in the pocket or on a key ring can be amazingly powerful.

On nights when the moon is bright you can usually see well enough to walk quite safely without the aid of a flashlight.

Some people take going out into the dark of the night quite naturally. They put aside their childhood fears of darkness, and learn to trust Spirit.

SCHEMATIC MAP OF THE SEDONA AREA

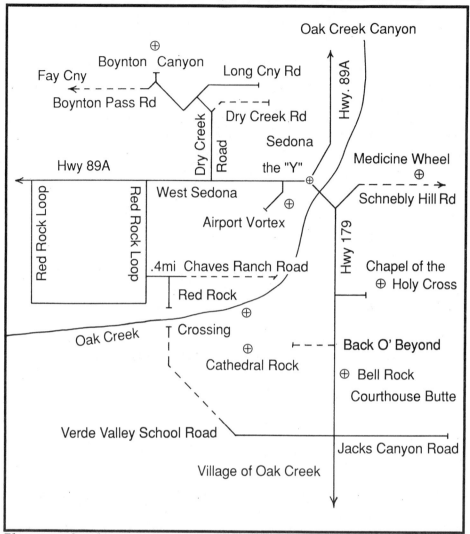

Please note that this map is not to scale, it shows only major roads, intersections, and places of interest. — All distances are from the "Y" - the intersection of highways 179 and 89a. All mileage figures are approximate. — Straight solid lines are paved roads, broken lines are dirt roads.

AIRPORT VORTEX - 1 mile. Take highway 89a West. Turn left at Airport Road. Go up the hill until you have passed the last house on the left. Park in any one of the parking areas. Always off the road!

BELL ROCK - 5.5 miles. Take highway 179 South 5.5 miles.

BOYNTON CANYON - 7.75 miles. Take highway 89a West to Dry Creek Road (3 miles) turn right. After 3 miles you will be at the intersection of Dry Creek and Long Canyon roads, turn left. Go 1.6 miles to next crossroad turn right. The parking lot for Boynton Canyon is less than half a mile from this last intersection.

CATHEDRAL ROCK - 4.2 miles. Take highway 179 East 3.2 miles to Back O' Beyond road. Turn right. Parking lot 1 mile.

IV

SEDONA'S PLACES OF POWER

On the left is Courthouse Butte; to the right is Bell Rock. Notice how the silhouette of Court House Butte resembles a Human face gazing skyward.

There are many beautiful and quiet spots along Oak Creek.

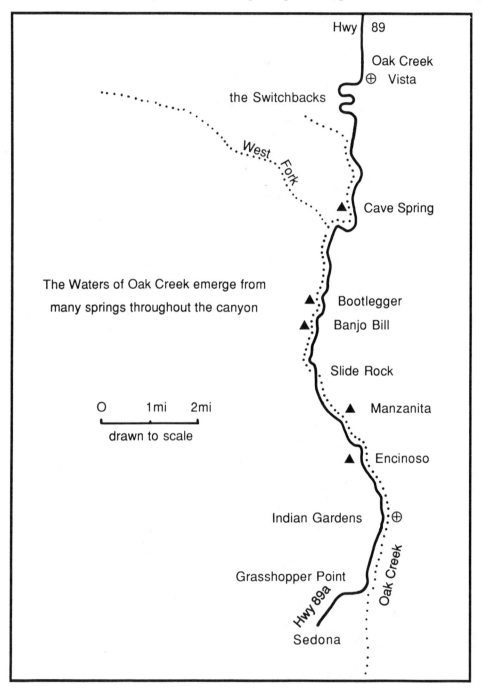

Hwy 89

Oak Creek
⊕ Vista

the Switchbacks

West Fork

▲ Cave Spring

The Waters of Oak Creek emerge from
many springs throughout the canyon

▲ Bootlegger

▲ Banjo Bill

Slide Rock

O   1mi   2mi

drawn to scale

▲ Manzanita

▲ Encinoso

Indian Gardens   ⊕

Grasshopper Point

Hwy 89a

Oak Creek

Sedona

A visit to Oak Creek may be the most healing experience that the Red Rock Country has to offer. Simply relaxing and letting go of our problems can be far more beneficial to our health and happiness than visiting a Vortex or Power Spot.

Shaman and mystics often spend a great deal of time clearing their thoughts before they attempt to work with Power. They know that when they open themselves up and become a channel for Spirit, their intent has to be clear or else there may be problems.

Before we visit a Vortex or other Power Spot, we need to relax and let go of our troubles. Not only can our negative emotions become amplified and projected back out into the energy field of the planet, but these energies can also pollute the energies of the Power Spots as well.

⊕ ⊕ ⊕

Quiet spots along the creek are ideal places for Spiritual, emotional, and mental rejuvenation. Healing currents of Earth energy are found where water flows freely upon the Earth.

WATER IS SACRED, WATER IS LIFE

Water has been well known for ages as being very sacred, and healing, not just to the body, but to the soul. Always respect places of water; we are born of water, and we are water.

The Master Jesus was baptized in water. That baptism was more than symbolic: It was a cleansing of the aura.

It is not always necessary to actually get into water to benefit from its healing powers. Just spending time near the water can be healing, especially if a person goes there with the intent of letting go of their problems.

FIVE MEDITATIONS FOR THE CREEKSIDE

1. Do a color meditation. Concentrate upon the green color of the trees, breathe in the color with each breath. Green is the color which stimulates the Heart chakra. This exercise is both energizing and energy balancing. (See both the Airport Vortex section, and the color meditation section for more information about this type of meditation.)

2. Listen to the water with your eyes closed, concentrate upon sensing nothing but this sound - the song of God. This meditation balances the left and right side of the brain.

3. Watch the water. As each thought comes into your mind, let it go into the water.

4. Lay upon the sand, the soil, or a comfortable rock and feel your connection with the Earth. This exercise can be done lying upon your back, or lying face down. If you do this exercise lying face down you may have the distinct sensation that energy from your Solar Plexus is moving down into the Earth and merging with the energy of the Mother. If you put your forehead to the Earth you may feel that you can actually project your consciousness into the rocks. This exercise is very healing, and "grounding."

5. While you are in the water concentrate upon feeling its healing energy.

⊕ COURTHOUSE BUTTE ⊕

Courthouse Butte is the formation a few hundred feet East of Bell Rock. Due to a mapmaker's error in the 1920s, Courthouse Butte is often confused with the formation near the creek at Red Rock Crossing, called Cathedral Rock. Old timers will tell you that these two formations are "named backwards." This misnaming continues to be a source of confusion. For the sake of clarity this guide book uses the names for these two formations as they appear in "official" Forest Service maps. Please see the maps in this book. Courthouse Butte is a Power Spot and a place of mystery. However, it should not be confused with Cathedral Rock.

From many locations around the Sedona area we can see that the entire summit of Courthouse Butte appears to form a silhouette of a Human face staring skyward. This monumental image awakens our sense of mystery and mythology, beckoning those with a sense of adventure to explore beyond the "veil"....

We know that the shapes of the rock formations of Sedona are constantly changing, and that we can see many figures in these rocks. Someday the face on Courthouse Butte will be gone. But for those of us who are here today, who are drawn to Sedona to learn the ways of the Earth, this face is a sign that the Spirit of the Earth resides in the Red Rocks. It is a symbol of the mythos and the mystical, mysterious "other side."

The "veil" that separates us from magical reality is very thin in Sedona.

This is why the Red Rocks seem mysterious. The energy of the Earth here allows us to come very close to contacting the "other side" of Sedona — the "enchanted landscape."

The magical Spirit of Sedona is that of the Earth itself. We are drawn to Sedona because this is a place where the Spirit of the Earth has always communicated with her children. The Spirit of the land calls out to our inner natures, asking us to remember our magical connection with the Earth....

Pay careful attention to your dreams while you are in Sedona. The Spirit of the Earth often communicates with us through our dreams. These "power dreams" form the link between our conscious mind and the unconscious mind, which remembers that the very essence of our being is one with the Earth.

The mysteries of our existence are hidden deep within our minds. Is life not a dream? And does the dreamer not awaken to find that once again they are dreaming?

(See picture on page 41)

THE REMAINS OF ANCIENT AMERICAN DWELLING PLACES

Many people who are interested in re-establishing their connection with the Earth feel a mysterious primal bond with the Native Americans and their culture. This connection with the past draws many people to the ruins of ancient native dwellings.

There are hundreds of so-called "archaeological sites" in the Sedona area. These "sites" may simply be small piles of rubble, or extensive structures such as Montezuma's Castle and Tuzigoot. I cannot however, in good conscience give directions to any of the archaeological sites in the Red Rock Country. Describing the location of any particular site in this book will guarantee that it will simply become too popular...after awhile there would be nothing left to see.

I feel that those who are able to find these places on their own will be also be the people who will be most likely to respect them. I encourage those who explore this enchanted land to keep their eyes open. If you are aware of your surroundings it is quite likely that during your explorations here you will find some type of archaeological site.

If you find a "ruin" please:
Take no souvenirs, move no stones, leave nothing behind.

PLEASE SEE THE PHOTOGRAPH ON PAGE 52

Recently, there has been a lot of what the Forest Service calls "vandalism" at various archaeological sites around Sedona. Without going into detail about some of the particularly low conscious things that have been done at and to some of these places, I will simply say that not only is any altering of ruins wrong, it is also very inconsiderate of the other people who would like to enjoy the ruins now, and in the years to come. How can anyone think that their spiritual quest requires them to alter things which were built by the Old Ones, and which can never be replaced?

Montezuma's Well and Tuzigoot are maintained by the National Park Service; check your maps. Montezuma's Castle is near Montezuma's Well...about 25 miles.

⊕ BELL ROCK ⊕

Of the "four major Vortices" Bell Rock and Boynton Canyon have generated the most stories and draw the most attention. However, the myths surrounding these two Vortices often fall in two distinct categories: Planetary and interplanetary. The mythology of Boynton Canyon revolves around the long standing legend of the Earth Goddess who is said to live there. People who feel that they are drawn to Boynton Canyon above all others, tend to be "Earth people"...those who feel a strong connection to the Earth. Bell Rock, on the other hand, is rather popular with the "cosmic adventurer" types, who look beyond the Earthly realm. Perhaps the most commonly shared myth about the Bell Rock Vortex is that it is somehow being used by extraterrestrials as an interdimensional portal\contact point with our time space reference.

INFINITE SOURCE OF CREATION

The word "Vortex", brings to mind the image of a swirling cone-shaped mass of energy...The spiral form of the Vortex is the blueprint for energy fields throughout the Universe.

Of the "four major Vortices" in Sedona, Bell Rock is the only one whose physical appearance resembles the form of the classic Vortex: Bell Rock is cone shaped...However, it is not shape alone which draws our interest to Bell Rock....

Bell Rock is a dynamo of cosmic energy. We think of it as "Earth Energy" because of our ground level view of the Universe. The energy field from which the Bell Rock Vortex draws its power is part of the unified field of energy that exists throughout the Universe. Here on Earth it is focused by our planet, and channelled through Bell Rock.

I believe that there is a large quartz crystal below Bell Rock, that has been naturally formed by Volcanic activity. And that this crystal acts as a energy transducer, focusing the Energies within the Earth and producing the Vortex.

At Bell Rock we are within the "Eye of the Vortex." Bell Rock is one of the primary focal points of the "energy grid" of electromagnetic Earth Energy which connects many Power Spots around the planet together. This energy grid - which the Native Americans sometimes call "the Web" - is an electromagnetic field in our biosphere that affects all life forms on the planet. This field of energy can be thought of as the nervous system of the planet, carrying information for the Group Mind of the Human Race.

Energy is information. We can receive information through this system and project thoughtforms into it (thereby "programming the energy"). So when you meditate, *please* remember to send out some energy in the form of prayers for peace and the healing of our planet.

⊕ ⊕ ⊕

Think twice before you pray to, or worship Bell Rock. There is only one true God in the Universe, and while all things are God, it is a mistake to worship the rocks which God hides behind...Enjoy the illusion...

Many serious Vortex explorers feel that there is a strong "groundwave" of energy circulating around the base of Bell Rock. It is this powerful groundwave which most people experience when they visit this Vortex.

This energy flow is rather distinct. It does not take special talent or extensive training to sense it or to work with it. There is a meditation technique in this section which should help you easily "tune in" to the groundwave.

It is because of the strong groundwave of Earth energies emanating out from the base of Bell Rock that it has become a popular place to conduct Medicine Wheel ceremonies.

The energy at the summit of Bell Rock is of a much higher intensity than that of the base. As the Vortex Energy spirals up around Bell Rock, it gains velocity and frequency, forming an "energy beacon."

The top of Bell Rock is a place of the Eagle Spirit, the Spirit of the Sun. This means that the powers of the summit can help a person contact higher realms. It is a good place for warriors to go to, asking for blessings and protection.

Merging with this energy flow can be a very powerful experience that can permanently alter the course of your life. This will not happen by "accident". A person has to ask the Power for help....

If you ever get to the top of the rock, stand up straight and tall and give your prayers to the Universe. Do not be afraid to ask for Power. If your motives are pure, and you are seeking the Power and knowledge of a warrior of the light, your abilities will be matched.

Many people speak of Bell Rock as being an "energy beacon"... One of my wildest fantasies about the Bell Rock Vortex is that there are two distinct flows of energy swirling around the formation...Being wide at the base, and tapering upwards past the summit, they twist together like the double helix of the DNA molecule, disappearing into infinity....

Beyond all the fantasies and illusions, the most important thing about Bell Rock, is that many people can feel its power.

Our Auras become synchronized with currents or fields of Earth energy automatically. The energy field around Bell Rock is so strong that it can actually be "felt", or rather...sensed with our minds.

With a little training and work, you too should be able to "tune in" to the energy of this Vortex, possibly experiencing an altered state of consciousness which may help you along your spiritual path. Directly experiencing this sort of energy can be very beneficial for the beginner, because it gives them "the feel" of working with the energies of pure Spirit.

If we allow it to, the field of Earth Energy at Bell Rock is capable of radically changing our energy structure and altering our state of consciousness. Meditating on these energies can be a powerful experience for everyone. The meditation described here is a metaphysical exercise that increases the meditator's strength and abilities. This type of meditation has been known to trigger paranormal experiences which frequently have a positive transformational effect upon the psyche.

This meditation is a Swirling Energy Meditation. Please read the meditation section of this book for more details.

This meditation alters the energy pattern of the body. Those who have read Carlos Castaneda's books, particularly the *Eagles Gift, The Fire Within,* and *the Power of Silence,* will perhaps have an easier time understanding the hows, and whys of the "energy shift" which is referred to in these books as "shifting the point of awareness."

This meditation can be done either sitting or standing. As usual, you should practice calming yourself with regular breathing before you actually begin.

Establish your connection with the Earth by giving yourself mental instructions to "become connected with the Earth."

Focus your intent on "tuning in" to the energy of the Vortex. After a few minutes of meditation many people will be able to feel this energy flow.

Say these words out loud; **"I am connected to the Earth, our energies flow together."** Use your "mind's eye" to visualize energy flowing both in and out of the energy center (chakra) at the base of your spine, and through the soles of your feet...Visualize yourself as an energy channel between the Earth and the Sky.

While you continue breathing steadily...Visualize the energy of your Aura merging with the energy of the Vortex..."See" and feel the energy flowing clockwise around you. (From left to right as it travels in front of you.)

After you have done this for a period of time which feels comfortable, invoke the energy with a spoken prayer such as this: **I invoke the power of this Vortex to clear away energy blockages in my system, and I invoke the power of this Vortex to awaken my psychic abilities.**

There is no need for me to give you advanced instructions for this meditation...Energy is information. As you "tune in" to these cosmic energies you will receive guidance... Your "inner voice" will tell you what to do.

As you do this meditation many thoughts and images may enter your mind; perhaps even images from past lives. *Ride the waves.* Concentrate on sending your consciousness into the energy

After you have meditated for a while, and you feel "well tuned," it is then a good time to pray for help, guidance, and for the healing of the planet.

When you are have become "well tuned" by meditating on the energies of the Earth, it is an excellent time activate your psychic center with a crystal.... Place a quartz crystal to your forehead, and focus upon that place known as the "Third Eye"...If you have the right crystal you should feel an energy sensation when you apply it to your forehead... Your psychic center is being activated.... Beginners should not do this for more than about fifteen seconds. (Or it may "overload" your circuits.)

Working with the energy of Bell Rock can be a catalyst which removes blockages in your personal energy field and opens your psychic centers. After your meditation at this Vortex you will hopefully continue to experience subtle changes that lead to higher levels of consciousness and increased psychic abilities.

A FEW BASIC IDEAS AND PRINCIPLES OF WORKING WITH EARTH ENERGY

Those who want to truly understand the Vortex experience must spend time meditating and practicing "tuning in" to the energy.

It is not surprising that many people visit Vortices and report "feeling nothing." Merely visiting a Vortex is not usually going to have any noticeable effect upon a person, other than helping them feel good.

Vortex energy is subtle. Those who want to truly understand the Vortex experience must spend time meditating and practicing "tuning in" to the energy.

Beginners can learn how to "tune in" to Vortex energy by first giving themselves the mental command to "become aware" to the energy. A mental command such as this invokes the Will.

Will is perhaps the most potent power that each Human possesses. Every action that we undertake begins as an act of Will. Don Juan called Will; intent. Many of Don Juan's teachings were designed to help Carlos understand that Spirit is directed by intent. Don Juan also taught Carlos that it was impossible to fully understand either Spirit, or intent. Instead we should allow these things to work without our thoughts getting in the way. So rather than looking for logical explanations, let us allow ourselves to be open to new experiences.

BEGINNER'S VORTEX MEDITATION

Spend a few minutes relaxing, then practice taking proper breaths. After you have relaxed, quiet your mind, and then give yourself the mental command to sense the energy, or to merge with the energy of the Vortex.

Even though you may think that you do not know how to do this, I can assure you that every person knows how to work with Spirit. This knowledge comes to us from the intuitive level, the place of silent knowledge: the I AM.

When the mind has become quiet you should begin to sense the energy of the Vortex. As you start to merge with the energy you may find that your meditation seems deeper or stronger than usual. You may also find that it becomes easy to enter an altered state of consciousness, or that you may begin to have the sensation that the energy around you is pulsing, or moving in waves. You may also be able to sense Earth energy by holding your hands out in front of you, parallel with the ground. This may give the sensation of "energy."

A simple invocation such as this can be used to awaken Spirit within a Vortex or any other Power Spot:

I invoke the Spirit of the Earth to guide me, and fill me with its power.

Or you could try something a little bit more far out, such as:

I call upon the light of the Great Spirit to enter my energy system, clearing away blockages and activating the proper light channels which will allow me to work with the power of Spirit.

CHANTING "OM"
BRINGS US INTO HARMONY
WITH THE SOURCE OF CREATION

The ancient mystics from whom we have inherited so much metaphysical wisdom understood that all things are energy, and that every form of energy has a frequency...a vibrational rate. These early philosophers referred to all vibration as sound. Traditionally, schools of Yoga and mystic wisdom have taught that the universe itself produces an endless sound. Which we call "OM".

Those who are on the spiritual path find that chanting simple syllables such as "OM" helps them integrate their personal energy fields with the Universe.

A short chanting session can have a very noticeable effect upon one's state of mind. Chanting opens up our psychic centers and balances our energy patterns.

Chanting in a Power Spot can amplify the power of our chant. Even those who have little experience in these matters find that ceremonial chanting at a Power Spot can expand their consciousness considerably.

Chanting in a Power Spot can be an important part of our initiation into the mysteries of the Earth.

Here in Sedona, we like to go to the places of the rocks and chant OM. This sort of chanting serves to "wake up" and balance the energies of the Earth, as well as the energies of those doing the chanting.

Earth healing ceremonies such as the Medicine Wheel should have a chanting session before or after the opening prayer. This helps to bring the group's energy into harmony.

To feel the power of the sound OM, one needs only to chant it correctly for a while. Intoning the OM is an art: If you are not taught how to do it properly, it is hard to understand exactly how it is done. When you chant OM, it is not really as if you are saying OM at all. The sound is OOOOOOOOOOOOMMMMMMMM The muscles of the Solar Plexus should be used to project a resonant sound throughout your space.

By properly chanting OM, the whole body is made to resonate harmoniously. Therefore our energy becomes balanced, and we are able to open up to the higher forms of psychic energy that are available.

Most Americans will feel a little silly when they first start doing this chant; that is ok. Chanting is not a basic part of our culture...yet...

If you came up on a group of people who were trying to chant OM, but doing it incorrectly, you would think that they looked a little silly. If you came up on these same people a little while later, and they were chanting OM correctly, you might wonder what planet they came from....

Electromagnetic waves of Earth Energy occur at frequencies (vibrations) just below the range of Human hearing. By chanting OM we are able to resonate with harmonic overtones of the Earth Wave...Chanting OM helps us to "tune in" to the Earth Energy.

51

It can be quite inspiring to find even a very small trace of an ancient dwelling. Such "artifacts" help us understand who we are and where we came from.

The cliff pictured here has two clefts in it which are typical of places in which "Indian ruins" are found (look closely). If you see something that looks like ruins and you would like to visit them, look for a trail that branches off the main trail, which seems to head in the direction you want to go. **Please stay out of the brush.**

⊕ BOYNTON CANYON ⊕

Boynton Canyon is considered by many to be the most sacred and magical place in the Red Rock Country.

There is a "mysterious presence" in the Canyon which cannot be properly described with words... When visiting Boynton Canyon many people experience what Yogis and Mystics refer to as deja vu... The feeling that one has been to this place before... It is as if the canyon were the landscape of dreams.

When gazing at the rocks one often feels as if the enchanted landscape was almost within reach; experiences of the waking world seem to merge with the reflections of the shadow world. The memories of dreams and events of the past often return, taking on new significance.

Casual visitors to Boynton Canyon will of course sense the mystery of this place, but to most it will always remain just that; a mystery. Only those who respect the sacredness of Sedona, and who are spiritually aware, will be able to experience her inner secrets.

There are tremendously mysterious things going on in Boynton Canyon which are barely hidden behind the "veil of illusion" known as reality: The key to understanding Boynton Canyon is that it is a place of Spirit; it is not merely a Vortex of energy.

Boynton Canyon is a place of initiation into the mysteries of the Earth. Spend time there praying and meditating upon contacting the Spirit of the Canyon. If your prayers come from the heart, and they are not ego directed, you may experience an initiation\activation, which will awaken your psychic abilities and strengthen your Spirit bond with the Earth.

This "activation" may be extremely subtle...occurring on the inner planes, but if you continue to build your power and study, you may look back on your visit to Boynton Canyon and see that you were in a truly magical, enchanted place. That you did contact Spirit, and that your prayers had a definite life changing effect.

After your visit to Sedona, keep working on yourself; meditate with your crystals and pay attention to your dreams. Learn to listen to your inner voice.

Those who have studied the mysteries of Boynton Canyon know that this canyon is a "twilight zone", a "crossroads", an "in-between place", where Spirit makes itself known to the beings of the physical plane... If you visit this Canyon remember to tread lightly; you have entered a magical place. Have respect for the Spirit of the Canyon...your actions there can produce effects that may last for your entire lifetime.

Native people and Shaman have a mystical view of the world; the world is a magical place...Even the most mundane event has vast significance...The Shamanic world is a world of superstition... Great care is taken not to insult "the Spirits."

The local Indians do not go on casual hikes in Boynton Canyon. To them this place is sacred ground that should only be visited in a very solemn ceremonial way.

The Yavapai Indians, who lived in the Sedona area for many generations before the whites came, have a traditional teaching that a powerful Earth Spirit; a Goddess, lives in Boynton Canyon.

And while no one outside the Tribe has access to their secrets, I believe that it is safe to assume that these Indians contacted this entity through Shamanic practices.

That is to say, by purification, fasting, meditation, and ritual the Indians were able to contact the Spirit of the Earth, which manifested itself to them as a "Goddess"...a supernatural being....

The legend of the Goddess in Boynton Canyon is particularly intriguing to those who believe that the shift towards planetary awareness and global healing is dependent upon humanity's becoming aware of the feminine Spirit of the Earth.

⊕ ⊕ ⊕

The Boynton Canyon Vortex is a blend of two distinct energy fields of magnetic and electric Earth Energy.

The entire canyon is a magnetic Vortex, the energy field emanating from the roots of the mountains themselves.

The primary focal point of the electrical Earth Energy is a rock spire near the mouth of the canyon, which locals have named the "Kachina Woman."

Since the effects of electrical Vortices are often much more pronounced than magnetic Vortices, the Kachina Woman has become a place that many people think of as "the" Power Spot.

Those who visit the Kachina Woman will know that they have found a truly magical space. You need go no further than this place in order to experience the canyon.

The area around the Kachina Woman is an ideal place to offer prayers to the Great Spirit, and the Spirit of the Earth. By using the energy of the Kachina Woman to activate your mind, you should be able to "tune in" to the more subtle magnetic energies which are present in this canyon.

Magnetic Vortices work upon deeper levels of consciousness than electrical Vortices. This is one reason why Boynton Canyon seems so mysterious; its magnetic field helps us access deep levels of the psyche.

Simply stated, those who wish to contact the Spirit of the Earth should enter a state of meditation with their intent (Will) focused upon that task....

Quartz crystals are excellent guides for this type of work. Not only do they help us "tune in" to spiritual energy, they also can be used to help us return to the canyon during dreamtime....

Quartz crystals are controlled by the Will; they can be programmed by mental, or verbal commands: Simply tell the crystal what you want it to do: If you want it to help you tune in to the Spirit of a Vortex, let it know. If you want a crystal to help you return to a place during your dreams; tell it that is what you want.

When choosing a Power Spot, simply look for a place that "feels right." After you have spent some time at this spot, ask yourself if you feel any different than you did before you sat down. Do you feel the same as you did a little while ago? Do you feel better, or worse? Have your thoughts changed? Do you feel calm, agitated, sleepy, at ease?

Do you think that the spot which you have chosen has an energy which affects your mind? And if it does, does this energy agree with you?

If the spot you have chosen doesn't feel right after you have been there awhile, or if you suddenly find yourself thinking negative thoughts, try another spot.

Many people do not realize that the world of Spirit holds many dangers as well as rewards. Those who do not take precautions are leaving themselves open for psychic attack.

Any time that you do any sort of meditation or other metaphysical work anywhere, it is a very good idea to pray to your guides and masters, asking them to protect you.

In Boynton Canyon it is particularly important to be aware of the fact that if you go into a deep meditation or have an out of body experience, you had better be protected with prayers, crystals, and the basic technique of shielding yourself with protective light....

Frequently visualize a protective white or golden light surrounding yourself... After awhile this shield will become a regular part of your Aura.

During regular meditations our energy field often expands, and this can be a good thing. But you should remember that if you do not call your energy back and ground yourself you will lose Power. So when you have finished meditating remember to give yourself a "mental command" to call all your energy back into its normal position around your body. At this time it is also helpful to focus your attention on your Earth connection, allowing yourself to become "well grounded."

The second most common myth about Boynton Canyon, after that of the God-dess, is that there are some very special crystals hidden in the Earth, below the Canyon. Many people have received this information during their meditations, or in their dreams. Various "channels" have also referred to the existence of these crystals. It is certainly within reason to believe that various types of crystals could have been naturally formed throughout the Sedona area during the time of the volcanoes. Crystals such as quartz are formed by the superheated water which accompanies volcanic activity. The "Crystals of Sedona" have not yet been turned into a tourist attraction...No one that I know of has seen them with physical eyes... At this point they only exist in the mythic realm. But this certain-ly does not mean that they do not exist.

SCIENCE FICTION ?

Energy is information: The energy matrix of the Earth is the planet's conscious-ness... Everything within the Earth's "gravity shell" is part of the planets informa-tion matrix.

Quartz, and other crystals in the Earth, help control the energy matrix of this planet. This crystal, energy\information matrix is a "Living Crystal Holographic Computer."

Beneath Boynton Canyon is a crystal cavern...one of many scattered throughout the planet. These types of Crystals are "Record Keepers"...the light codes of the planet are encoded upon their crystal matrix.

When the Living Crystal Holographic Computers of this planet become com-pletely activated, all light and consciousness on this planetary sphere will become integrated.

At the present time this system's functions are somewhat limited to autonomic control of planetary systems, and as a memory bank.

It awaits the time when certain members of society become conscious of its existence and awaken it with their mental energies. Total activation will not hap-pen in one generation.

The Human form originated upon this planet as an inter-galactic light code (morphogenetic field), which became part of this planets information\energy matrix... Light codes control the development of physical bodies through the DNA molecule.

Our consciousness is directly linked to the planet's information\consciousness matrix...Humanity's social\memory complex (group soul) is imprinted upon Record Keeper Crystals, some of which are below Boynton Canyon.

The Shamanic practice of "contacting the Spirit of the Earth" allows us to "tap in" to the information\consciousness matrix of the planet.

Native American Shaman contacted the Living Crystals of Boynton Canyon. It was in this way that the Goddess " was awakened."

The Goddess is the planet's reflection of the Human light code. The light code is in no way affected by the realities of mundane physical existence; it is a emana-tion of the divine mind of God. This is the mystery of the Canyon... At one time or another many of us have been there in spirit. Our light codes are encoded upon the energy pattern of the Crystals.

Everyone who visits Boynton Canyon will of course notice the resort development at the mouth of the canyon. This resort is known as "Enchantment." The Enchantment is a world class resort which caters to well to do people.

When this development was first proposed, the Sedona metaphysical community was of course quite upset... How could anyone be so greedy and out of touch with their spiritual natures as to build a hotel on sacred land?

Many dire predictions were made. The most commonly expressed thoughts about Enchantment were: The developers would go bankrupt. And that someday the resort would become a great healing center.

As many people predicted, Enchantment did run into financial difficulties. The financial problems which Enchantment experienced were largely due to the arrangement that the developers had with their bank... The savings and loan which financed Enchantment went belly up, taking Enchantment with it....

Since then there have been several groups which have tried to buy Enchantment, and rumor has it that at one time a Japanese company considered turning it into some sort of an amusement park! Fortunately Enchantment has found new owners who seem able to handle the responsibility of managing such an important property. I had a short telephone conversation with one of the owners, Dr. Barbara Breitbart, who informed me that she and her husband do not plan major changes for the resort. They have, however, added a special health and fitness program to the resort's amenities.

Dr. Breitbart is a psychologist, and she assures me that she is interested in all aspects of the Human experience.

While the intentions of the original developers may appear to be somewhat questionable, it is important to remember that Boynton Canyon is a place of Spirit, and as Don Juan told Carlos: It is impossible to understand Spirit; instead we should allow Spirit to do its work, and accept the results as they manifest themselves.

Enchantment may well turn out to be a great blessing for both our planet and our species. As the group consciousness of Humanity makes its shift towards planetary awareness, the Enchantment resort will have an opportunity to play a key role in awakening the Earth bond of many people who are in a position to directly affect banking and industry.

Each person on our planet has the opportunity to make the vital decision to begin healing the Earth. Those who are not wealthy can work to heal the Earth by doing simple things within the boundaries of their daily existence. Those who command wealth, or who are in key positions in business or government, are able to affect society in ways that can have far reaching consequences.

A visit to Enchantment may help to re-awaken the spiritual nature of people who are in a position of power, who will be able to do things which will help heal our planet, and bring mankind together.

This resort was built on a small piece of private land surrounded by national forest. The first white people to hold title to this property homesteaded it as a cattle ranch.

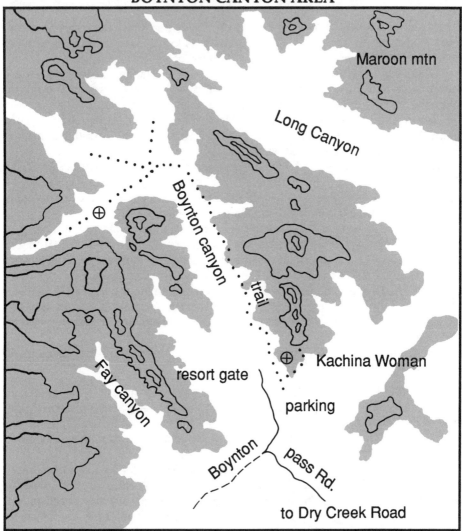

Maroon mtn

Long Canyon

Boynton canyon

trail

Fay canyon

resort gate

Kachina Woman

parking

Boynton

pass Rd.

to Dry Creek Road

Boynton, Fay, and Long Canyons are box canyons. The trail which leads into each Canyon is also the trail which leads out of that canyon. By simply following these trails you shall find beautiful places.

If you see a small group of "real looking" Indians in or around Boynton Canyon, do not photograph them, approach them, or try to talk to them, unless they speak to you first. They may have come to work their "medicine," and may not want to be interfered with. In fact, out of respect for their tradition you may want to leave the canyon entirely.

As you wander down the path into the heart of the canyon you will notice a private residence built upon the Enchantment property which resembles a Moslem temple. (At one time the dome was painted blue.) The management of Enchantment tells me that this structure is a private home, it was not built by an Arab, and it is not a mosque

Hiking can be a distraction that keeps the consciousness fixed upon the physical world... It is only within the stillness of the quiet mind that one is able to experience the mysteries that lay beyond the veil...

THE KACHINA WOMAN

The entire Canyon is a magnetic Vortex. The deeper one goes into the Canyon, the deeper they travel into the womb of the Mother, until at last they find themselves in a place where the physical and the spiritual meet....

⊕ ESTABLISH A MAGICAL SPACE ⊕ FOR POWER AND PROTECTION

Whenever we meditate, alone or in groups, it is helpful to consciously establish a "magical space" which we may think of as a private temple. Establishing and entering a magical space separates us from the ordinary world. When we are in the temple we are meditating, praying, and performing ceremonies. The magic circle can also be used to protect those who are within the circle from undesirable outside influences.

We can create a magical space in our homes or any other place where we happen to be. The basic exercise for establishing a magical space is to simply claim the space which you are in, and visualize protective white, or golden, light coming into your Aura from just above your head, filling the space around you.

Many people who are seriously interested in working with the Power of Spirit use physical objects to establish their magical space. These physical objects can be simple things such as a circle scribed into soft soil or drawn with corn meal, or the circle can be made of elaborate layouts of crystals, stones, etc.

Mystic traditions vary, but we do know that the circle is the most basic form which we can use to mark the boundaries of the magical space. The two most significant variations of the basic circular form are the six pointed "Star of David," and the five pointed Pentagram. (Why is the military center of the U.S. a five sided building?)

If you are serious about exploring the realms of deep meditation or astral projection, you should always remember to establish a magical space around yourself at the beginning of your meditation.

If you are practicing these things at home you may decide to establish a permanent temple arrangement in the place where you usually meditate. Begin each session with a prayer for guidance and protection, and then use the protective light visualization.

If you are attempting to practice astral projection or deep meditation at a Vortex area it is a good idea to establish a magical space as you meditate. But after you are done, you must also remember that it is important to "unmake" your magic circle. If you do not unmake your circle, another being may come along and tap in to, or otherwise disturb your energies...this can cause real problems. After you are done with your meditation or ceremony, use the power of your Will to call all of your energies back into their normal position, using your Earth connection to ground yourself. And then physically unmake your circle.

Establishing a magical space with physical objects can be very beneficial in helping empower our meditations and ceremonies. However, the person who does this must remember to not allow themselves to get overly fixated upon their ceremonial objects...

⊕ AIRPORT VORTEX ⊕

The Airport Vortex is the most accessible Vortex in the Sedona area. It is an Electric Vortex, and its energy is some of the most easily felt, but you must remember that this "electricity" does not strike like a thunderbolt; it is subtle force which affects the mind and body from within.

Many people who visit this Vortex, whether they are metaphysically oriented or not, will agree that they can sense the "electricity in the air." This is another way of saying that one feels good, and full of life. Feeling good is the body's reaction to Electrical Vortex energy.

Since it is so easy to experience the energy of the Airport Vortex, it is an excellent place for beginners to go in order for them to "get the feel." As one works with this Vortex, their bodies' energy level will increase. This will energize both the Central Nervous System and the subtle energy system in much the same way that Yoga exercises are known to do, thus allowing one to experience the altered states of consciousness which are associated with psychic phenomenon.

Working with the energies of the Airport Vortex, or any of the other Power Spots around Sedona can be a catalyst that helps awaken psychic abilities. This does not mean that we have to depend upon the energies of a Vortex in order to find the proper atmosphere for meditation. Once we have had our initiation at a Vortex we should be able to begin to fly on our own...

⊕ ⊕ ⊕

The Airport Vortex is not on top of Airport Mesa. In other words, it is not at the top of the mountain at the same level as the airport. It is located about half way up the hill. (See photograph on page 33.)

To reach Airport Vortex; simply go up Airport Road, off Highway 89. After you pass the last house, which is near the road on the left, look for a place to park (off the road).

All the parking spots along the road are close to the Vortex. You should have no problem finding a trail which will lead you to the Vortex area in less than five minutes.

What you will find are two small hills that have a steep gorge at the base of their West side. **This area is charged with Earth Energy.** Several trails crisscross the area, connecting all the "Power Spots" together. Any trail you take will lead to an interesting place. Where you go is just a matter of personal preference, and guidance.

There is no singular place of Power at the Airport Vortex. There are, of course, several places which are recognized as "Power Spots," and you will know them when you see them. One way you can tell these things is by how well traveled the trail leading to the spot appears to be, and the other way is by noticing how the land is shaped....

The Vortex occurs in the area of the "two small hills." The energy field is bipolar, being divided into two "lobes" around the two hills and the gorge at their bases. From the area of the cliff that runs along the base of the hills, you may get the impression that the Vortex itself is actually hanging in midair, just beyond the cliff, above the gorge.

The area right between the two small hills is considered by many to be as close to the "Eye of the Vortex" as a person can get without actually being able to float in midair above the gorge....

Perhaps the best place to encounter the energy of this Vortex is at the summit of either of the two small hills. Electrical Earth energy tends to travel up through the Earth until it reaches the summit of a mountain, hill, or other formation (such as a spire). It is then discharged into the air. By "tuning in" to the energy being emitted from these hills we find harmony with the Spirit of the Earth.

The easiest trail to the quiet inner part of the Vortex area runs along the top of the cliff, between these two hills. If you encounter a Medicine Wheel somewhere along the ledge that forms the cliff that this trail travels over, you have found a good place to offer a traditional gift of tobacco or corn to the Earth.

The large hill just to the North the Vortex and the "two small hills" is recognized as a place of Power. There are at least three Medicine Wheels at its summit. Local legend has it that one of the three Medicine Wheels at the top of this hill was there before the first white settlers arrived...

The energy of the Airport Vortex is ideally suited for awakening our psychic abilities; perhaps the most effective meditation technique which we can use to take advantage of the energies at this Vortex is the Sunset meditation. This type of meditation is very powerful; I recommend that wherever you live you find a place where you can regularly meditate on the light of the Sun.

Yoga Masters often recommend Solar meditations and color meditations because they are so beneficial for balancing and energizing the energy system of the Human. Meditating upon the Light is the way of the Rainbow Warriors. These meditations stimulate the "Third Eye" (the pineal gland). This gland, which is located near the center of the brain, is known to be the sensory organ of telepathic communication, "spiritual vision" and other "paranormal" powers.

In order for you to understand the meditation which is given on the next page, you should read the section in this book which describes the theory and practice of color meditations in detail.

PRAY FOR THE HEALING OF THE MOTHER EARTH

WARRIOR'S SUNSET AT THE AIRPORT VORTEX

The summits of either of the two hills at the Airport Vortex are particularly good places to watch the Sunset...

The Sunset meditation is a very simple, yet powerful technique. If this meditation is done correctly, you will feel an immediate energy boost and experience a heightened state of consciousness which can help you "go within" to meditate and pray.

The key to this meditation is to gaze towards the West and concentrate upon absorbing the colors of the Sunset. (**Never looking directly at the Sun itself.**)

To do the Sunset Meditation get to the place where you are planning to meditate well before the Sun actually sets, allowing yourself plenty of time to calm down before you actually begin to meditate.

Once the Sun has touched the horizon, it takes a little less than five minutes for it to disappear. This gives us a definite time span for this meditation: Everyone should be able to hold their attention for five minutes.

You may either sit or stand to do this meditation. Be sure to focus part of your consciousness on your connection with the Earth; this will complete the energy circuit between the Sun and the Earth, thus lowering your resistance to the high energy light communication that you are preparing yourself to receive.

SOLAR LIGHT MEDITATION

1. Breath through the nose, using the muscles of the abdomen to drawn in your breath.

2. Feel your connection with the Earth.

3. As you watch the Sunset, give yourself a mental command to "absorb" light energy through your eyes. (This activates the Will... once given the command your Will shall do this automatically for you whether you understand it or not.)

4. Every time you take a breath, visualize yourself absorbing Light Energy. "See" this light energy flowing through your body; from your Third Eye to your Solar Plexus.

5. As you breath in, visualize the light energy going into your forehead as it is drawn into your belly. When you exhale, visualize the energy flowing through your body and out of your forehead.

6. Close your eyes and concentrate on your Third Eye, "seeing" and feeling light energy from the Sun entering your system through your Third Eye. Keep breathing; keep the energy circulating.

7. Alternately open your eyes, drinking in the light with your eyes and with your breath. Then close your eyes and "see" the light of the Sun with your Third Eye.

8. **Do not look right at the Sun; gaze toward the West.**

As you gain power by doing this meditation, your psychic abilities will become awakened. Light meditations are one of the most direct routes to higher consciousness. You will find answers to questions that many people never learn to ask....

There is literally no limit to the benefits of this type of light meditation. By practicing regularly, you may someday become a Master of light.

ESTABLISHING YOUR ENERGY BOND
⊕ WITH THE EARTH: ⊕

WE ARE THE RAINBOW BRIDGE

As you do Sunset meditations or any other meditations, it is important to establish your bond with the Earth. This completes our body's natural energy circuit with the planet, and in fact, completing this "circuit" is a very powerful and energy balancing meditation in itself... Try simply meditating upon being a channel which draws energy into the Earth.

Every Human Being has a natural energy connection with the Earth. Our primary contact points with the Earth are the soles of our feet and the base of our spinal column. If we want to explore the world of Spirit, it is very important to strengthen these connections with the Earth. Without good Earth contact people become ungrounded, "floaty," and unable to control their energies.

When you want to work with Earth energy you should use the Power of your Will to consciously reinforce your "Earth connection." Do this by visualizing "roots" coming out from the bottoms of your feet and the base of your spine, "see" these roots with your minds eye, going deep into the Earth, connecting you firmly to the Mother. Use your power of creative visualization to "see" energy traveling up from the Earth into your feet and the base of your spine... This exercise helps you to establish a firm Earth connection.

Another powerful form of this meditation is to draw energy into the Earth. This connection completes the circuit between our Father Sun and our Mother Earth, making the person who completes this circuit a "Rainbow Bridge." This type of meditation energizes and balance the energy of the meditator.

For serious meditation on the energy of the Earth, the feet should be bare. This enhances your contact with the Earth, and helps subtle energies of Spirit flow through your system in the manner nature intended... The classic position for working with Earth energy is standing. The body becoming a "grounding rod."

Another excellent way to strengthen your energy bond with the Earth is to put as much of your body as possible in contact with the Earth: Lay face down upon the soil, the sand, or a rock and feel yourself merging with the Earth.

This is very effective and you may find that if you invoke the power of your Will with the "mental command to "merge energy with the Earth" you will have the sensation that your energy centers at your Third Eye and Solar Plexus will send out "feelers" into the Earth...

This exercise will balance your energy. And it can be done before or after any other meditation.

⊕ CATHEDRAL ROCK ⊕

Cathedral Rock is the most famous rock formation in Arizona. The image of these sandstone towers casting their reflection in the water is perhaps the ultimate statement of Sedona's visual magnificence.

It is not easy to describe the presence of Cathedral Rock. From afar, it is impossible to tell what mysteries the heights have to offer. It is certainly one of the most amazing spaces that I have ever experienced.

Cathedral Rock is a Vortex proper, and there is no mistaking the power, or the presence there. It is a very sacred place, and it should be approached with respect.

Local legend has it that a Master of the Spiritual realm works with the energies of Cathedral Rock, and that this master is there to help people who come to that place seeking spiritual guidance and healing.

Cathedral Rock is known to be a place of Dream Activation.

Many people have dream time experiences that are triggered by the energies of the "rock." You do not have to *be* in Sedona to dream Sedona. Perhaps the most magical place of all is the land of dreams....

⊕ ⊕ ⊕

High on the west side of Cathedral Rock (facing the creek at Red Rock Crossing) there is a formation that acts a channel for the Earth energies. It is the type of formation that is known to geologists as a basalt intrusion. Basalt is an iron bearing type of Lava.

Cathedral Rock is known as a magnetic Vortex. This is because the basalt intrusion near the center of the formation is composed of iron; therefore, it draws magnetic energy from the planetary energy field, thus producing a field of biomagnetic Life Force Energy.

Cathedral Rock is a magnetic Vortex... A magnet does not just draw particles to itself: It also sets up a magnetic field, drawing the space around itself into order. Magnetic alignment is a prime quality of this Vortex.

A Magnetic Vortex should never be called a negative Vortex. The word negative has an unfortunate double meaning....

Some teachers refer to the Cathedral Rock Vortex as "negative," because it draws energy...incorrectly comparing this Vortex to the negative pole of a battery....This improper use of electrical terms gives us a very poor verbal model for describing this Vortex.

In the case of Cathedral Rock, the word negative certainly does not mean that this is a "bad" Vortex. The magnetic field of this Vortex is not de-energizing. In fact, due to the principle of induction, we can "pick up" energy from this Vortex.

Magnetic fields such as this Vortex also balance the energies of the body. Our bodies' electrical system automatically resonates with the subtle magnetic field of the Earth. At a magnetic Vortex such as Cathedral Rock the natural energy of the Earth is stronger than most other places, therefore it is particularly easy to "tune in" to the balancing and healing energy field of the planet.

Magnetic resonance with the Earth's energy field is a desirable state that occurs naturally to all beings upon the planet. Vortex explorers have found that the strong field of the Cathedral Rock Vortex can supply a boost which has very desirable effects....

At Cathedral Rock you are in an energy field that allows you to become very connected and in tune with the Earth. Establishing a strong connection with the Earth is very important to everyone's spiritual development. By "tuning in" to this field of energy, and resonating with it, you will experience a re-alignment of the energy field of your body which can be very beneficial to your overall health and well being, as well as your state of consciousness.

Working with the magnetic Vortex can have a lasting effect; the energy field works directly upon the Human energy system. A person who "tunes in" to this Vortex can receive a "new program"... especially if they are willing to change and let go of undesirable "old programs."

This "reprogramming" (light activation) happens both on the mental and spiritual levels. By resonating with these energies it is possible to experience activation of dormant circuits of the central nervous system which interface with the energies of the "higher planes" and are associated with paranormal abilities such as ESP, telekinesis etc.

It is important to remember that one trip to the Vortex will only accomplish so much...Whatever circuits are opened up must be worked with regularly at home in order for them to become properly developed.

There are Power Spots all around Cathedral Rock. Many of us who work with the Vortices here in Sedona refer to certain features of the land as temples, or altars. Each dome, spire, and grotto seems to have its own special energy.

There is a standing wave pattern of magnetic energy around Cathedral Rock, and it is not necessary to climb all the way up to the area of the basalt intrusion or the base of the spires in order to "tune in" to the energy of this Vortex.

The amount of energy of the Vortex will vary from time to time, as will the strength and resonance of various places around the Vortex. Particularly notable will be monthly changes with the phases of the moon, etc.

To draw the energy in, it is helpful to find a place on the formation that is "right". The energy fields around Vortices are not stationary. So each time you visit a Vortex, you should practice using your intuition to find Power Spots:

You may simply find a place that "Feels" right. Another way is to use a Dowsing Rod, or the palms of your hands, to sense the energy flow.

Once you have found a spot that feels good to you, spend some time meditating upon the experience of just being there. Then use the power of your Will to "tune in" to the Vortex...simply giving yourself the mental command to "tune in" or absorb energy can activate your Will... And your Will has the power to perform the most amazing feats...

Cathedral Rock is an excellent place for Sunset Meditations. These meditations are described both in the Airport Vortex section and in the section on Color Meditations. If you meditate on the Sun at Cathedral Rock, I am certain that you will experience a powerful altered state of consciousness...I suggest you take advantage of every opportunity to absorb the sacred energy of the Sun.

This Vortex is a special place of spiritual healing and transformation. But in order for you to receive the full benefit of the Vortex experience your intent has to be pure. The clearer you are, the more powerful your experience will be.Vortices are not good places to take your mundane personal problems. It is up to you to use your own personal power to straighten your problems out. Angry emotions and energy from frustrated desires can create a "cloud" that pollutes the psychic atmosphere around a Vortex or other Power Spot.

If you are not clear (of negative emotions) the power of a Vortex might not be good for you...True Shaman take great care to empty themselves of negative energy before they attempt to contact their power...So please take the opportunity to "mellow out" before you visit any Vortex or Power Spot.

Water is well known among healers for its ability to cleanse both the physical, and the spiritual bodies. The creek area below Cathedral Rock is a place of healing, and a excellent place to let go of the things that are bothering you.

Many people will be far more healed by the waters at the base of Cathedral Rock, than any other place around Sedona.

Sedona is in the Coconino National Forest; therefore it is legal to camp nearly anywhere for a period of up to two weeks. Remember, fires are not always allowed (and often unnecessary). Pack out all garbage and bury all other waste.

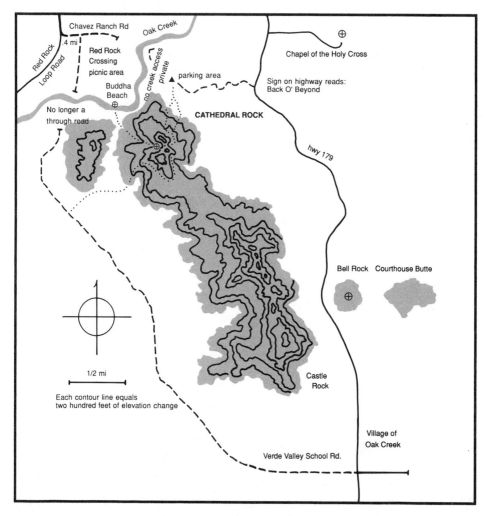

Each contour line equals two hundred feet of elevation change. Paved roads are marked with solid lines, dirt roads with dashed lines, trails with dots.

Please do not attempt to climb Cathedral Rock, or any other of the sandstone formations in the Sedona area unless you are an experienced hiker with some experience climbing, or you are with someone who does have experience.

Remember rock in the Sedona area tends to be crumbly. And rock on the sides of Cathedral Rock tends to flake off...the place you have decided to stand may come loose! So keep your eyes open, and your hands out of your pockets.

CRYSTAL DREAM CAVERN MEDITATION: A DREAM FANTASY MEDITATION

This dream fantasy can be done at a Vortex, or at home. You can have a friend read this meditation to you as you relax, or you can read it to yourself and use the ideas in this meditation to guide you in creating your own journey.

This meditation can be used anywhere you are. The energy boost of a Vortex can help you have the power to reach the crystal dream cavern. Or you can use the images of this meditation to help you reach Sedona from far away.

For powerful experiences in Sedona, or at home, use this meditation in conjunction with the dream techniques in this book. Try reading this meditation for several nights in a row, just before you go to bed....

It is helpful to pray to your guides and masters for guidance and protection before you do this meditation.

Relax, feel yourself merging with the waves of magnetic energy that are emanating from the rocks. Use the power of your Will to consciously tune in to the Vortex energy. Do this by giving yourself the mental command to "merge with the energy." Breathe deep, relaxed breaths.

You can feel that there is a source of radiant energy pulsing with power deep in the rocks below you. It is as if there were a tiny Sun within the rocks emanating warm inviting waves of energy.

Go within your mind and see yourself as if you were in a dream. Since you are now in the dreamtime and no longer limited to the rules of the waking world, simply Will yourself to move toward this warm radiant source of healing Earth energy that is sending its vibrations through the rocks.

Feel yourself passing through the rocks, their substance gently massaging your spirit as you move through them. As you project yourself toward the mysterious power source within the Earth you suddenly find yourself transported to the heart of the crystal cave.

The crystals of this cavern glow with a warm healing golden light, and you feel as if you were in an pleasant warm ocean of sparkling electrical energy. You are drawn to a crystal which fits comfortably in your hand. As you pick it up, a telepathic "voice" tells you that what you are about to partake in is the direct experience of God's divine radiant love.

The crystal begins to emanate warm pulses of electrical energy which fill your being with pure ecstatic joy. As this happens your energy centers open up and you become a channel of pure rainbow light energy as God's divine sevenfold beam of brightness and illumination awakens your energy centers.

As you become filled with this healing energy the entire cavern begins to glow with one particular color... which is it? Red? Turquoise? Violet? or maybe Blue, Yellow, or Orange? whichever color it is, this is either the color of your Power, or your healing.

Suddenly you find yourself back in your physical body. Lay there for a moment remembering your crystal journey, then give yourself the mental command to "become fully present in your body." Sense that all parts of your consciousness have returned to their normal waking positions. Open your eyes; awaken to the dream...

⊕ THE CHAPEL OF THE HOLY CROSS ⊕

The Chapel is a great monument to the power of the Christ.

The Chapel receives more visitors than any other Power Spot in Sedona. It has been a place of spiritual healing and guidance for many people who would never think of visiting a Vortex. There are many inspiring stories associated with this place.

It is most amazing that this beautiful temple of Christ has found its place so close to so many other Power Spots. This was surely meant to be.

The use of the Cross to symbolize the union of cosmic energies, and to mark a place of Spirit far predates the Christian era.

FIRE AND WATER

⊕   ⊕

THE SAN FRANCISCO PEAKS AND MONTEZUMA'S WELL

These two places of Power represent two rather distinct and seemingly opposite aspects of Earth energy. To the North of Sedona stand the San Francisco Peaks: ancient volcanos, a place of sometimes frightening power. To the South of Sedona we find Montezuma's Well, a place which invites all who visit to bask in the healing Spirit of the Earth Mother.

The San Francisco Peaks are a dominant force in the spiritual beliefs of the Hopi, the Navajo, and the Yavapai Tribes. These Tribes believe that powerful Earth and sky spirits (Kachinas) inhabit the area of these peaks. The natives do not take the Power of this place lightly, and great care is taken not to insult the spirits. It is recommended that these peaks be left in solitude.

As part of the basic premise of this book I have tried to explore the concept that energy is information. In the case of the San Francisco Peaks, we can see that the local Tribes have been attracted to, and have "tuned in" to, the same energies which many other groups of people on various parts of the planet have also "tuned in" to - Mythic energy - the group consciousness of the Human race, wherein the archetypes with which we create our Gods are found.

The highest of these four peaks is also the highest mountain in Arizona; **Mount Humphreys (12,643 feet). The canyons of Sedona are carved into the feet of the mountains which are crowned by the San Francisco Peaks.**

⊕ MONTEZUMA'S WELL ⊕

As children of the Earth we are born into this world with a spiritual bond to the Earth which draws us to enchanted oases such as Montezuma's Well. The legends of the Human Race refer to many places such as this; "sacred wells," places of healing, where the spirit of Man is touched by the caress of the Earth.

Legend has it that there is a system of caverns in the Sedona area which extend at least as far North as the San Francisco Peaks, and as far South as Montezuma's Well. the "sinkholes" of Sedona and Montezuma's Well are places where these caverns have broken through to the surface.

Clans of both the Hopi and Yavapai Tribes have a traditional teaching of a time when they lived within the Earth (after the destruction of their original homeland), eventually emerging through Montezuma's Well and the Grand Canyon.

These clans feel their emergence from the Earth was the birth of their people into the new world. It is because of this legend, and the fact that this is obviously a sacred place, that Montezuma's Well continues to be visited by several Tribes of Native Americans who draw out water for ceremonial purposes.

Schnebly Hill is part of the "Rim" that defines Oak Creek Canyon. Its summit is part of the highlands of Central Arizona (also known as the Colorado plateau).

Schnebly Hill is another area which is subject to a certain amount of name confusion. At this point everything we can see from Sedona which is between Schnebly Hill and town is referred to by many as "Schnebly Hill." This includes the canyon leading up to Schnebly Hill and the group of rock formations that stand between Schnebly Hill and town.

It is these rock formations in particular which many people think of as Schnebly Hill. For the sake of being accurate in my writing I will refer to these rocks as the "Schnebly Hill Formation." (You may notice that some maps of this area refer to the Schnebly Hill Formation as the Mitten Ridge.)

The Schnebly Hill Formation is the rather prominent Red Rock formation that stands 'alone' at the mouth of Oak Creek Canyon, across from Wilson Mountain and Uptown Sedona.

The Schnebly Hill Formation is a Place of Power and Spirit. So many people have come to recognize this area as a Power Spot that it has become common to hear it referred to as the "Schnebly Hill Vortex." During the time of the Harmonic Convergence many people gathered on a large flat formation in the middle of the canyon which leads up to Schnebly Hill. They constructed a large Medicine Wheel on this formation which is approximately one hundred fifty feet across. Since then this Medicine Wheel has been the focal point for many Earth healing ceremonies. Many people who have traveled to Sedona remember their visits to this Wheel as one of the most magical, spiritual, and healing experiences of their lives.

Although this Wheel is recognized by Sedona locals as a sacred sight (as it is), the Forest Service periodically threatens to tear it down.

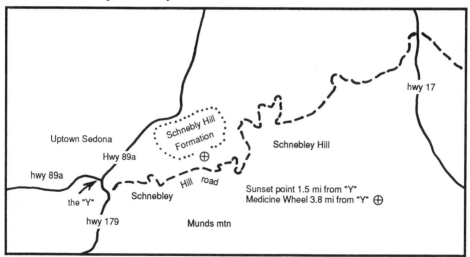

Capitol Butte is one of the most prominent mountains in the Sedona area. Due to its location, it can be seen from miles away, making it the first part of the Red Rock Country that many people see as they head toward Sedona on Highway 179 from Phoenix.

Capitol Butte, like Wilson Mountain and Bear Mountain, is a "sentinel peak." A prominence that is in such a location as to have a commanding view of the countryside. Such places are always considered to be places of Spirit.

Psychics, Channels, and Dowsers tell us that Capitol Butte is a major energy center. In fact, several ley lines (lines of magnetic force) converge at Capitol Butte.

This should surprise no one who takes the time to note Capitol Butte's position on a map. Capitol Butte (and the two other mountains previously mentioned) are right on the edge of a major geological feature, the Colorado Plateau. Capitol Butte occupying a central position between Wilson Mountain and Bear Mountain, thus becoming a natural place for Earth Energies to converge.

Capitol Butte figures rather prominently in the mythology of Sedona. Some believe that Capitol Butte is "the" Vortex, the "hub" of the Sedona energy grid, endowed with energy that seems to emanate from large and powerful crystals that are within the mountain. Perhaps the wildest Capitol Butte myth is that there is a crystal temple within Capitol Butte that was established by the Lemurians. I do not expect you to accept that story as absolute fact. We will just have to wait and see....

Dreamers in the Sedona area often report having dreams of underground chambers and rivers. There is also great deal of speculation about the existence of underground cities or temples in the Sedona area. If they do in fact exist, then they may be found in the area around Capitol Butte, Wilson Mountain, and Dry Creek.

CAVERNS BELOW SEDONA

The sinkhole in Soldiers Pass (between Capitol Butte and Wilson Mountain) is proof that subterranean water has carved caves through the sandstone foundations of the Red Rock Country.

Many of us who enjoy speculating about Sedona mythology say that the sinkholes in the Sedona area may actually be places where the entrance to these caves may be hidden...

⊕ THE COCKSCOMB / TREE FARM ⊕

Cockscomb is the "western gate" of the Enchanted land. This Power Spot is sometimes referred to as "the Tree Farm".

The Cockscomb is visible from many places in West Sedona. As you drive west down Highway 89, it appears to be the last Red Rock formation on the western horizon.

In the years to come we will hear more about The Cockscomb. What is a little surprising is that until recently there has been little recognition of the Cockscomb as a Power Spot. I suppose this is due in part to the fame of the Major Vortices. People do not always have the time to explore other places...they flock to the places that are tried and true.

The Cockscomb occupies a very significant position in relation to many of the other Power Spots and Vortices in the Sedona area.

Holding its position at the first major turning of Dry Creek as it makes its way into Oak Creek, the Cockscomb is an ideal receptacle for the Earth Spirit as it flows along the ancient waterway of Dry Creek...Dry Creek is a channel for underground water, therefore it is also natural path for Earth Energy.

Besides being a natural place for the Spirit of the Earth to reside, the Cockscomb is also in geographical alignment with several other notable Power Spots around Sedona. This would indicate to those who are interested in geomantic principles that the Cockscomb is a rather notable formation in its own right.

It is an interesting to note that the Cockscomb, Cathedral Rock, and Bell Rock can be plotted on a straight line. These three formations form a line across the landscape which defines the Western boundary of the Red Rock Country. When we extend this imaginary line past the Cockscomb, it runs along the base of the mountains on the opposite side of Boynton Canyon, finally terminating at Loy Butte, near Sycamore Pass. This is one of the most significant geographical alignment of landforms in the Sedona area.

Imaginary lines drawn across the land do not necessarily mean anything. We have to be able to discern whether alignments have occurred by random chance, or if they indicate a true geometrical projection of the divine form. (Remembering that Geometry is one of the three laws that control the forces of creation. The other two laws being Math and Music.)

NOTES ON BEING A SPIRITUAL WARRIOR

Wilson Mountain as seen from Uptown Sedona.

⊕ WE WALK THE RAINBOW PATH ⊕

There is a Spirit in the Earth which unites all beings: We are one with the Earth, and while our inner spiritual nature has never changed, our external shell of emotions and beliefs has slowly taken us away from our source.

By the time the White Race arrived in the new land we had already lost contact with our true spiritual source. We no longer listened to our inner voices, instead we had begun following a false set of rules which are contrary to the laws of nature. We overwhelmed the Red Man because they lived by natural law. They had not a hope against our twisted logic.

And now the time has arrived when the blindness of the White Man threatens to destroy all life upon the Earth. But as we stand on the brink of destruction we once again begin to awaken to nature's voice....

The Native Americans have preserved the medicine visions of great Indian Chiefs and mystics which foretold of this time. Perhaps you have heard of the Hopi prophecies, or the vision of Black Elk?

These prophetic visions have a common theme of a time to come when men who are blind to the sacred nature of the Earth would defile her so entirely that all life would be threatened. But as the time approached when it seemed that all hope for survival would soon be lost, a generation of great teachers and healers would arise who would have the power to undo the damage that had been done to the Earth. And the wisdom to bring all beings on the planet together in love and harmony.

The Native American mystic Black Elk spoke of the path which we must take in order to heal the Earth as the Rainbow Path, the path of light. This is the mystic path which leads to direct realization of the Great Spirit and to harmony with the forces of nature. Many of us who are drawn to Sedona are walking the Rainbow Path.

We are the Warriors of the Rainbow: We who hear the call of the Earth asking us to remember our mystical natures, realizing that we are not merely creatures of flesh, but also creatures of Spirit, beings of light walking the mystic rainbow path between the Earth and the sky.

We must take responsibility for our lives. We must learn how to become powerful. And as we grow, the Great Spirit and our Mother the Earth will speak to us and tell us what to do.

We are beginning to learn directly from the Earth itself: By meditating and using crystals which help us to "tune in" to the energy of the Earth, amplifying our thoughts and powers.

With power comes responsibility. Our actions should become like that of a master and so we become impeccable warriors of light.

To be a Rainbow Warrior, your first responsibility is to save the Earth. Your second responsibility is to save yourself. You must become a keeper of knowledge. And you must become Zen... beyond knowledge.

We are Warriors of the Rainbow, we have returned, we shall re-awaken the energies of the Earth, even as the Earth is working to re-awaken us.

In the year 1986 a ship which bore the name Rainbow Warrior was sunk by a bomb which had been planted by an agent of the French government.

At the time of the bombing the Rainbow Warrior was docked in New Zealand, being prepared for its return to the area of the Pacific ocean where the French test atomic weapons in the atmosphere.

The ship Rainbow Warrior is owned by the international ecological protection group Greenpeace. The mission of the Rainbow Warrior was to occupy the French test sight in order to prevent the French from detonating another hydrogen bomb in our air.

The ship was sunk, killing one crew member, and the tests continued. The man who bombed the ship was caught by New Zealand authorities, and eventually turned over to the French (who later released him)....

The Rainbow Warrior went to the bottom of the bay, but she did not go down in defeat. She only spent a short time below the waves until She was raised to the surface and repaired. The Rainbow Warrior still rides the waves on the front lines of the eco-war.

WHAT ARE YOU DOING TO HELP SAVE OUR PLANET?

Each on of us must make a stand, wherever we are.
We must save the rainforests, the oceans, and the air or all will be lost.
Learn to conserve all resources. We can no longer afford waste.

VOTE

The White House Opinion Poll (202) 456-1111

Greenpeace USA 1436 U Street, N.W., Washington D.C.20009

Sierra Club 730 Polk st., San Francisco, Ca. 94109

Rainforest Action Network 301 Broadway suite A, San Francisco, Ca. 94133

Environmental Defense Fund 257 Park Ave South N.Y. N.Y. 10010

SELF OBSERVATION IS THE KEY TO CONSCIOUSNESS

Many of us who are on the spiritual path find that the philosophy of Zen provides some of the best guidance and insight into our own beings and our place in the Universe. Zen is based both upon the teachings of the Buddha and the ancient Chinese teaching of the Tao (pronounced "dow").

The Tao is a natural philosophy for understanding our existence. We are told that the word Tao means "the Way." The ancient sages from whom we have inherited the teaching of the Tao understood that the entire Universe is a great Wheel which can be understood by observing its cycles. Understanding "the Way" (learning to work with the Tao) brings one's life into harmony with the Universe.

Zen meditation leads to the direct understanding of the Universe. It is the path "beyond knowledge." When one practices Zen meditation they empty their mind of thought... When the mirror of the mind is clear, it reflects the Universe....

The Zen concept of "no mind" (beyond knowledge) echos Carlos Castaneda's teachings of Don Juan... Carlos was told repeatedly that he had to "stop his internal dialogue" in order to be able to work with Power. (With silent knowledge.)

The spiritual warrior trains their mind so that it becomes more conscious of itself and its place in the Universe. It is a paradox; as the student becomes aware of their own consciousness (ego) they merge with the Universe, and therefore transcend the ego: Becoming less conscious of the self, and more conscious of the Universe.

Having a well balanced ego is one of the keys to consciousness expansion. By noticing your intellect, you have become self aware. Therefore you are tuning into the Universal Mind, the very powerful "I AM" presence.

The more a person is able to identify with themselves, and the more they are able to observe their own mental processes, the better that person should be able to understand themselves and the way they organize their thoughts. This results in the student becoming more aware. Their actions become less automatic, and they stop simply "re-acting" to their environment with basic animal behavior: They become a warriors.

The more a person is able to realize that they are part of the Universe, and that they are the Eyes of God, the more "in tune" with the I AM presence they become.

As a person becomes more "in tune" with the Universal Mind (the I AM) the circumstances surrounding their lives will become harmonious. Planetary and national karma allowing, they will become somewhat "luckier." And they will be able to follow their Spiritual paths: Things will happen for these people instead of to them.

Karmic debts always have to be paid. The idea is to create as little karma as possible. And as you work out whatever karma you have accumulated, try not to create any more.

This is done by acting firmly and correctly. Think of yourself as a Spiritual Warrior who must survive the tests of the world.

⊕ NOTES ON BEING A WARRIOR ⊕

To be a Rainbow Warrior is to be a magician who works with the energies of the Earth and the Light of the Great Spirit. Using the power they have gained to transform themselves and the Earth.

As Warriors on the mystic path we have the opportunity to become self aware and learn how to balance our energies. We can learn how to live in harmony with the forces of nature, letting the energy of the Universe work for us.

We must learn to live our lives as an example of strength and correct action. We must seek the Truths of spiritual knowledge which help us see through the illusion of the world that we have created.

While other members of the clan pursue "normal lives" the Spiritual Warrior breaks away to pursue the mystic path.

A Spiritual Warrior 'sacrifices' experiencing many of the superficial things that society expects of its members. A Spiritual Warrior knows that the desire for "things," such as fancy cars, expensive jewelry, etc. is just a trap which keeps many people from realizing who they really are, and what they should really be doing.

Many Spiritual Warriors find that they have to sacrifice being accepted by their social group. The Spiritual Path is the way of the few, not of the many. No one else can walk your path, and sooner or later you must break away.

Often times Spiritual Warriors must also break away from their own families. They must realize that their truths, and their path, is more important and more valid than that of their parents, or anyone else....

Therefore, a Spiritual Warrior must sometimes feel the pains of loneliness. But these pains pass away, and as a Warrior becomes stronger the things they were once lonely for cease to be important.

BECOME A POSITIVE SOCIAL THREAT! SET EXAMPLES! LEAD THE WAY!

DO NOT WORRY WHAT OTHER PEOPLE MIGHT THINK

YOU MUST ACT CORRECTLY, EVEN IF IT GOES AGAINST THE GRAIN

A WARRIOR MUST DO WHAT A WARRIOR KNOWS IS RIGHT

If there are not any WARRIORS in your town, RECRUIT SOME.
AND REMEMBER:
IT IS VERY ZEN TO SAY THAT A WARRIOR MUST BE ABLE
TO LAUGH AT THEMSELVES!!!

VI

MEDITATIONS FOR DEVELOPING
PSYCHIC ABILITIES

⊕ COLOR MEDITATIONS ⊕

The art and science of color meditation has been practiced for thousands of years by Yogis and Mystics. The ability to "work with light" is the most valuable skill a Human Being can master. As the Master Jesus said: "I Am The Light." All those who work with light are establishing a bridge between themselves and the highest spiritual beings in the Universe. Not all forms of light can be seen with our physical eyes....

Color meditations will quickly open you up to the direct experience of metaphysical Light energy (Prana). You will be working with Light energy that comes directly from the Sun; your mind and body will become energized and spiritually healed. "Light programs" contained within the genetic code and nerve structure are activated... Psychic awareness is increased.

Color meditations serve to balance the energy of the body and awaken the body's energy centers. These energy centers are known to us by the ancient Sanskrit word; Chakra.

The seven Chakras of the Human Aura, and the energy channels that run parallel to the nerve channel of the spinal column, are often referred to as the "Rainbow Bridge."

Each Chakra is associated with a gland in the physical body. These glands are transfer points (transducers) between the non-physical realm of the light energies and the physical body. When a Chakra is stimulated it causes a gland in the physical body to secrete hormones which are "trigger mechanisms" that alter the body's chemistry and lead to altered states of consciousness....

The higher Chakras, which are located in the brain, are the energy centers which serve as our contact points to the higher realms of consciousness. When activated these energy centers work with the Pineal and the Pituitary glands, which are our physical organs of "extra sensory perception," capable of sending and receiving signals of pure light energy.

Our "Third Eye" psychic center, the pineal gland, works with our "Solar Plexus" to absorb, circulate, and control energy (otherwise known as light) throughout our body.

"Solar Plexus" is a proper medical term: A Plexus is a place where blood vessels or nerves come together and intertwine. The Solar Plexus is the center of the Human body. Since ancient times it has been known to be our body's center of vitality and connection point with the Solar Mind. The Solar Plexus is located just below our rib cage in the center of our body. Proper breaths are drawn through the nose with the muscles of the abdomen and the Solar Plexus... Breathing through the mouth dulls the mind...

Color Meditations are always done with breathing exercises. Oxygen that has been charged by the Sun is taken into the body with the breath. The action of the breathing muscles of the Solar Plexus circulates the light force energy through the body.

THE SEVEN CENTERS OF HUMAN CONSCIOUSNESS

⊕   The Pituitary Gland is associated with the energy center at the top of the head, the seventh Chakra. This Chakra is known as the Crown Chakra. It is the crossover point between the physical body and the Soul. Soul Consciousness is associated with this Chakra.

⊕   The Pineal Gland is your "Third Eye." It is sometimes referred to as the magic eye. Stimulation of this gland leads to ESP (perceiving non-physical energy as information). This gland is able to absorb light energy, even though it is located deep within the brain. This is because these higher forms of light energy exist in an energy state that is more refined and quite beyond the physical.

⊕   The Throat Chakra is a powerful energy center. Its gland is the Thyroid. The Throat Chakra is associated with Sound (vibration). In metaphysical terms, sound is one of the primary energies of the Universe. With our voices we "create" sound energy. Sound moves matter.

⊕   The Heart Chakra is the center of our energy system. Its gland is the Thymus. The Heart Chakra helps balance the lower primal forms of Life Force energy with the higher forms of light energy.

⊕   The Solar Plexus is the body's center of life giving vitality. It works with the Adrenal Gland. It is know to Mystics and Yogis around the world as the seat of the Will. According to the system of the Native Americans, it is the center of our being.

The Solar Plexus works with the Third Eye to draw light energy into our system. When you do Color Meditations, focus on your breathing. As you breathe, visualize light energy circulating through your Third Eye and your Solar Plexus.

Your Solar Plexus is known to radiate and absorb energy. This is very well described in Carlos Castaneda's *Tales of Power*. Strands of light fibers (Akashic Threads), which exist on the etheric plane, radiate from our Solar Plexus and connect us to the world. Jose Arguelles refers to these fibers in his book *The Mayan Factor*, as the "Umbilical Cord of (*or to*)the Universe" the Kuxan Suum.

⊕   The energy center below your Solar Plexus is associated with the Spleen and the Ovaries. This Chakra is a basic Life Force center and is important to the general vitality of the organs in the lower body. Strength in this energy center is necessary for controlling out of body experiences.

⊕   The Root Chakra is located at the base of the spine. It is associated with the sexual organs. The Root Chakra is your connection with the Mother Earth and Her primal Life Force energy. Some of the most potent forms of Yoga concentrate on awakening this energy. This energy is known by the ancient sanskrit word; Kundalini.

⊕ WE ARE THE RAINBOW BRIDGE ⊕

The Chakras correspond to the seven rays of color.

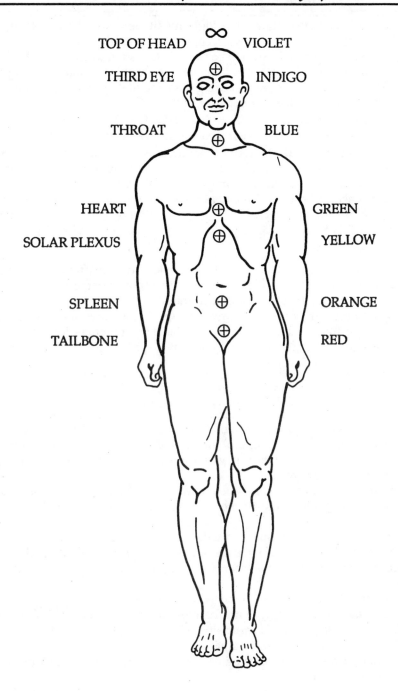

TOP OF HEAD   ∞   VIOLET

THIRD EYE   INDIGO

THROAT   BLUE

HEART   GREEN

SOLAR PLEXUS   YELLOW

SPLEEN   ORANGE

TAILBONE   RED

There are two basic forms of color meditation: Those which focus the meditator's mind upon specific colors, and those in which the meditator concentrates upon becoming "aware of the light."

When we do color meditations and Light meditations we become Rainbow Warriors. Illumination occurs when we become filled with the Light of the Great Spirit. As we become illuminated, our bodies become strengthened and healed. The true purpose of our life is revealed to us and we are able to contact our higher selves; our Soul Consciousness. By practicing these meditations we are learning to direct Spiritual energy with the power of our Will.

COLOR MEDITATIONS, and LIGHT MEDITATIONS
These two terms are somewhat interchangeable

Generally, when we speak about color meditations we are talking about "open eye" meditations upon sources of colored light, or visualizations of specific colors. This is somewhat different from "becoming aware of the Light."

When one practices becoming aware of the Light, they focus their consciousness upon pure Spiritual energy as it is perceived by the Third Eye. The most potent forms of this Spiritual Light are perceived by mystics to be the White, Golden, and Violet Rays.

Simply "meditating upon the Light" is an excellent meditation for developing psychic awareness. With the eyes closed, one uses their power of creative visualization to "see" a white or golden light with their mind's eye.

This light enters our personal energy field from just above the head at the Soul\body energy transfer point (the eighth Chakra). Students of metaphysics know that this light is not imaginary; it is a very real spiritual force which Human Beings have the power to invoke.

The Chakras convert light to life energy.
Each color of the visible light spectrum stimulates one of the Chakras.

Many students of metaphysics find that meditating upon specific visual colors can be a very powerful energizing and energy balancing meditation. The basic form of the visual color meditation is given in the Airport Vortex section. (See Warriors Sunset at Airport Vortex.)

Perhaps the most notable color meditation is the Sunset meditation. Concentrating upon the golden light of the Sun energizes and balances the body's energy system.

Another powerful form of this meditation is to concentrate upon an intensely green light such as that given off by grass or trees in the full Sunlight. Meditating upon the color green stimulates the Heart Chakra, balances the energy of the Aura, and heals the body.

A powerful color meditation involves focusing our mind's eye upon each Chakra, one at a time, beginning with the root chakra. As each Chakra is concentrated upon the color which is associated with that Chakra is visualized flowing in and out of the Chakra with the breath.

An alternate form of this meditation is to visualize white or golden light flowing through the Chakras.

⊕ EXERCISES TO AWAKEN THE THIRD EYE ⊕

The Third Eye can be stimulated by applying "pressure" to it. This "pressure" is something that most people can learn to become aware of: By concentrating within your head on the area above and between your eyes. Some Yoga teachers would say to "gaze upward" with your eyes closed.

Your Third Eye is affected by breathing exercises. It works with your Solar Plexus to absorb and circulate energy through your energy system.

This meditation directly stimulates the Third Eye. Once the Third Eye is stimulated certain things begin to happen automatically. Listen to your inner voice. It will tell you what to do.

THIRD EYE MEDITATION

Relax while you sit up straight with both feet on the floor. Use your Will to make your connection with the Earth.

Take proper breaths through your nose, using the muscles of your abdomen and Solar Plexus to draw the air in. Relax.

After you feel that your breathing has become steady, let all your breath out and hold it. While you are doing this, focus on your Third Eye and concentrate until you really must breathe. Then you may go ahead and breathe.

This exercise will stimulate the Third Eye. You should feel "high" after this exercise.

After you start to become conscious of your Third Eye, you may experience physical sensations in that area of the forehead. This is natural, and it is good.

*Placing Quartz Crystals on the Third Eye
is an excellent way to awaken your psychic abilities.*

MEDITATION II
This meditation is similar to the first.

Sit up straight and make your "Earth connection."

Breathe properly, imagine that you are circulating energy with your breath.

Pay careful attention to the act of breathing. Notice the air going in, and out of your nose. Visualize the muscles of your Solar Plexus drawing energy into your body and circulating it throughout your system.

Think of the air as energy. Imagine that as you draw in each breath some of this energy is also being drawn into your Third Eye and energizing it.

After you do this for awhile, exhale completely and concentrate on your Third Eye. Go deep inside and apply "pressure" to your Third Eye

THE THIRD EYE IS THE ORGAN OF ESP.

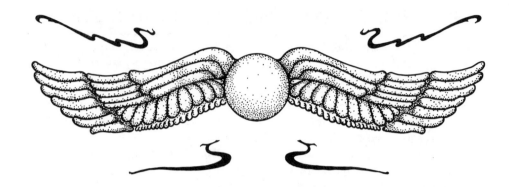

FULL MOON ENERGY

On nights of the Full Moon psychic energy is at its highest. We are told this is the best time to try to use Mental telepathy to contact the Masters of Light.

To experiment with telepathy, relax for a while and meditate, then just try to project your thoughts.

People who do color meditations, or other exercises to stimulate their Third Eye, will find that they can excite the Third Eye to the point where they actually can feel that they are projecting their thoughts.

Times of the full Moon are also excellent times to contact the Masters through prayer. When you pray to the Masters, it is especially powerful if you pray out loud....

TWO EXERCISES TO HELP US LEARN HOW TO
⊕   WORK WITH EARTH ENERGY.   ⊕

This meditation - visualization works especially well at Power Spots. During this meditation the meditator uses their natural ability to channel energy as an act of Will. The energy which is to be channeled through the meditator is sent forth to heal the planet.

This meditation is done lying upon the back...a suitable place must be found.

See yourself as an energy channel. Visualize the Golden Light of God's love entering your Third Eye and Solar Plexus. This energy activates your Central Nervous System.

See this energy flowing out from your body through your arms and legs, *forming a pool of golden liquid light around you.*

See this liquid light spill forth from the pool, finding and following the small watercourses and streambeds which wind their way across the countryside.

See this energy merge with the waters of the Earth in the nearby streams.

See the Light flowing with the water into larger streams and rivers, ultimately finding its way to the ocean.

See the ocean become filled with the golden healing Light of God's love.

See all this in your mind's eye.

Send forth the Light

TREE HUGGIN'

It is from the great Native American teacher, Sun Bear, that I learned this exercise. If you want to feel one with the Earth, hug a tree, it is very grounding.

Carlos Casteneda's teacher, Don Juan, tells us that with his ability to *see* the energy, *the luminosity* (the spiritual essence) of things, he can *see* that trees, and Human Beings have very similar energies. He told Carlos that some shaman work with trees, using them as their magical allies. The Celtic people also understood that trees have a special magic, or energy, which is very harmonious with the spirit of the Human.

Please treat the trees with respect, they are wise.

The trees will tell you the story of the land, if you will but listen.

You will find big pines deep in Boynton Canyon. Don't miss your chance to give one of them a long hug....

A MEDITATION OF
SWIRLING VORTEX ENERGY

Meditations using the swirling energy of the Human Aura have been used by students of metaphysics for thousands of years. There are many variations of the basic technique. Some of the names that are used to describe this type of meditation are: Etheric Vortex, Spiritual Whirlwind, and Cone of Power.

Swirling energy meditations allow us to directly experience the reality of our bodies' energy field, the Aura, as well as the "cosmic" energies from which we draw our inner strength. Developing awareness of our Aura and the natural energy flow of the Universe can be an important step leading towards the development of psychic powers.

Going deeply into a swirling energy meditation is truly a magical operation that cannot be properly explained in words. This type of meditation can clear unwanted or undesirable energy from our Aura, and it can also lead to an altered state of cosmic consciousness.

Swirling energy meditations are ideally suited for working with Vortex energies and the Medicine Wheel. Vortices can supply an energy boost which can accelerate learning, or increase the power of the meditation. Medicine Wheels provide a resonant form for group energies. Powerful thought projections which can affect the fabric of the Universe can be sent out from a Medicine Wheel that has been brought into harmony with a swirling meditation.

The energy field which is found to be most beneficial for Humans to work with travels in a clockwise direction into the Earth. This is the "way of the Sun." During this meditation you should focus your intent on the energy which is flowing in this direction.

As with all meditations it is important to relax for a while before you actually begin to do the meditation.

Breathing properly is very important: Remember that a proper breath is drawn through the nose, and the muscles of the abdomen are used to draw the breath in.

This meditation helps put us in touch with the natural energy flow of the Earth. It is therefore important for the operator to establish a strong connection with the Earth. This is done by giving yourself a mental command to "connect" with the Earth, and by visualizing this happening. Doing these two things activates our Will. (Which has the ability to control energy.)

Visualization and the use of Will are the "key" to energy meditations. Visualization is not merely imagining something happening. Visualizing is "seeing" something in your mind's eye and willing it to happen. The more you meditate and practice visualization, the more powerful and real your work will become.

Swirling energy meditations are usually done standing up with the (preferably bare) feet flat on the ground. You may stand with your legs either a little way apart, or with your legs together, depending on how you feel at the time. The knees should be relaxed. That is to say, the leg should not be "locked," the knees should be slightly bent.

⊕ SWIRLING ENERGY MEDITATION ⊕

1.   As you relax your breathing use the power of your Will to strengthen your energy bond with the Earth. Do this by concentrating on the soles of your feet and the base of your spine while you give yourself the mental command to "establish energy contact with the Earth". Feel this contact, feel energy flowing between yourself and the Earth.

Continue breathing deeply, and steadily.

2.   After you have established your contact with the Earth, use your natural psychic ability to "tune in" to the energy which swirls through your Aura as it makes it's way into the Earth.

3.   Begin by visualizing a Vortex of energy flowing around your body: It moves into your Aura from above your head and swirls its way into the Earth.

4.   Give yourself the mental command "tune in to this energy."... Tell yourself to "become synchronized with this energy which is flowing around me."

As you develop awareness of this energy flow you may find that you will have the distinct sensation that you can actually feel this energy moving around you. Developing this awareness is the first step.

The goal is to be able to become completely familiar with working with this type of Spiritual force so that you can "tune in," or "tap in," to it for its Aura purifying, and recharging qualities.

This type of meditation also alters the consciousness in a way that allows the meditator to project their consciousness along the threads of energy which weave the Web of Life.

Many people will find that they can easily get "way out there" by using this meditation. And that while they are way out there, they learn things that are beyond description.

The energy of Bell Rock is ideally suited for amplifying the meditator's ability to do this meditation, and to simply "get the feel."

This is one of the paths of Power.

WHEN WE HAVE DONE THIS MEDITATION, AND HAVE BEGUN RESONAT- ING WITH THE ENERGY OF THE PLANET, IT IS VERY APPROPRIATE THAT WE SHOULD USE OUR PRAYERS TO INVOKE SPIRIT, ASKING FOR THE HEALING OF THIS PLANET AND OURSELVES.

See pages 108 and 109 for more information

⊕ SOUND ⊕

Those who are interested in contacting the spiritual forces of the Universe and working with the energies of the higher planes can benefit greatly by learning how to use the power of the spoken word.

Matter moves Spirit: Speech is one of the most powerful tools we are given. Through the power of speech we are able to set matter in motion. We "create" energy with our power of speech.

Those who are interested in developing their psychic abilities will find that the power of the spoken word can become one of their most powerful tools for removing blockages and creating realities.

Spoken Prayers, Invocations, affirmations, and chants "program" the energies of the Universe. When words are spoken out loud, sound energy is "created," thus becoming a permanent part of the Universe...and the Universe has ears....

The spoken word also has the ability to program the subconscious mind. This programming can be used to help us get rid of unwanted habits, or to help us learn new ways of behaving.

An invocation is a statement that is worded so as to call something into being, or cause something to happen. The following statement is an invocation:

"I invoke the light of Christ to enter me, to cleanse and purify my heart."

Invocations are frequently "sealed" by statements such as; "So be it, and so it is." This is a statement known as an affirmation; it affirms your words and empowers your Invocation.

Affirmations which contain the phrase "I AM" are particularly powerful because they invoke the all present and encompassing I AM presence of God, the Universal Mind.

"I AM A CLEAR AND PERFECT CHANNEL OF LIGHT. I RECEIVE THE BLESSINGS AND THE PROTECTION OF THE GREAT SPIRIT. SO BE IT, AND SO IT IS."

Throughout our lives we are programming our subconscious. Much of the programming which we receive is social conditioning. Unfortunately, much of this social conditioning programs us to remain unaware of our potential as magical beings.

One of the best methods of re-programming the subconscious mind is through the power of the spoken word. By simply repeating certain carefully worded statements out loud, over and over again, we can reach the subconscious mind.

The subconscious Mind has a very powerful connection with the Superconscious Mind (or Soul Level). The Soul is recognized as the force behind our personalities as conscious beings. It is the "I AM" consciousness of the mind of God...the Universe experiencing itself. **This is the level of consciousness as pure energy.** In Carlos Castaneda's books this is known as the Nagual.

It is our highest goal in life to achieve the level of Soul consciousness (super consciousness). At the level of Soul consciousness we transcend the physical limits of our existence and merge with the energy matrix of the Universe.

Our conscious mind cannot understand the workings of the Soul Level, and we are correctly taught that it is a mistake to try to understand this level (the Nagual). We are advised to just accept its workings as they appear to us, out of "nowhere"..."like magic."

⊕ ⊕ ⊕

This chant is very powerful. It is designed to help you get in touch with your Soul. While you say it you should visualize your connection with the Universe... your eighth energy center... which is just above the top of the head.

As we work out our karma and we are able to align ourselves with the will of the Soul, our lives should become somewhat easier, and good things should start happening for us.

∞

THE SOUL MANTRA

I AM THE SOUL
I AM THE LIGHT DIVINE
I AM LOVE
I AM WILL
I AM PERFECT DESIGN

EXPLORING THE MYSTERIOUS REALM
⊕   OF DREAMS   ⊕

Dreams are our link with the world of pure Spirit. The realm of existence where thought is action. The dreamtime is the dimension where we learn that Will (intent) has the power to alter reality. Mystics throughout the ages have recognized the power of the dreamtime in helping them integrate magical reality with waking reality, knowing that if one can master their dreams they can transcend the limits of material existence.

Many people who read this book will remember having strange and powerful dreams. Many you have already begun to practice dreaming, and there are no doubt a few of you who are advanced students.

This teaching is primarily for those who have not yet practiced dreaming, or who seldom remember their dreams.

There are many techniques for becoming aware of our dreams. One of the first basics for bringing on power dreams is keep the body well-rested. If you work hard all day and go to bed exhausted, you are quite likely to fall into a deep sleep which will not allow you to return with any memory.

Dream masters also recommend that a person who is interested in exploring their dreams go without sex. This allows the body to store up vital life force energy which is then used to energize our nervous systems (and therefore increase our psychic abilities). When we go without sex, Life Force energy moves up through our system from our lower energy centers into our higher psychic centers, thus energizing them. This Life Force energy is also a vital element which gives us the power to remember our experiences in other dimensions.

This does not mean that you have to go without sex to have powerful dreamtime experiences and memories. Doing so simply increases the probability that you will have the Power to remember your experiences. Remembering is the task of the warrior. Everyone has amazing out-of-body dreamtime adventures several times a week. The "trick" is to remember them. For this task we need our Power.

It is important to remember that for most people sex is an important energy balancing factor. If one goes without sex, but does not use this energy for expanding their consciousness. their energies may become somewhat unbalanced.

People who do not have children should take note: If you would like to have the most astounding transcendental adventures and possibly become a true magician; avoid having children. Save all your power for yourself. [Read Castaneda's books.]

Other than simply conserving one's Power, prayer and intent are two of the most important tools which can help us in our quest. Be sure to pray to the Great Spirit, your guides, and Masters for help, protection, and guidance

If you want to explore the world of dreams and you want to increase the probability that you will have powerful experiences, try the exercises on the next page for at least five days in a row.

A FEW SIMPLE STEPS FOR AWAKENING THE DREAMER

1. As you go through the day remind yourself that you are going to work on remembering your dreams.

2. Get plenty of sleep: Do not stay up until you are exhausted.

3. Avoid having sex before you sleep.

4. As you drift off to sleep tell yourself that you are going to remember your dreams. As you do this concentrate on your Third Eye.

5. Linger in this nether state as long as possible and continue to concentrate upon your Third Eye as you tell yourself to remember your dreams.

6. Remember your dreams.

7. Buy a simple note pad and record your dream memories.

8. Think about your dreams: project yourself back into your dreams. Use your dream book to help you remember.

The "nether state" which we drift through as we go to sleep is a very powerful state of consciousness. At this time we are in an Alpha brain wave state and our minds are ready for "programming." At this time we can give ourself autosuggestions to do many things. We can tell ourselves to not eat so much, or that we do not need cigarettes. We can also tell ourselves to remember our dreams.

At some time during your dream experiences you will have a brief moment during which you will realize that you are dreaming. You will have made the link between your waking mind and your dreaming mind. It is at this time that you should try to bring your waking awareness along with you into your dreams.

At first you should not try to control your dreams. Merely watch them and then return with the memory. Later, you should begin trying to actually control your dreams. When you find yourself in a dream, begin dream control by giving yourself the mental command to see your hands. This helps establish a link between the waking world and the dream world. Many people I have talked to read this technique in Carlos Castaneda's books and later found that they could indeed find their hands in their dreams.

Dreamwork is a form of consciousness projection. Developing Power in dreams helps one learn to Astrally project and Soul travel. Those who are seriously interested in developing these abilities should lay down with their head facing North. In this position we are aligned with the energy flow of the magnetic field of the Earth as it travels from South to North: The energy of the Earth can help lift you out of your body.

The goal of these exercises is to establish the link between the nonphysical realms of pure Spirit and Will, and the consciousness of the waking world. However, the beginning student is advised to always make a purposeful and complete transition from one realm to another. Never "jump up" from a deep meditation. Instead the dreamer should slowly feel themselves becoming fully integrated with their body, giving themselves the mental command to be fully present in their body.

If one does not make a conscious and purposeful transition from one state to the next, two things can happen: Parts of one's being may become lost in another plane. Or a person may simply damage their ability to enter magical reality. The beginner's logical mind needs a definite separation between realities.

VII

VORTEX MYTHOLOGY

X MARKS THE SPOT.

REMNANTS OF ANCIENT CIVILIZATIONS INSPIRE TODAY'S SEEKERS OF TRUTH

Today's religions and metaphysical teachings have their roots in the teachings and the mystery schools of the prehistory civilizations of Atlantis and Lemuria.

While many establishment scholars try to deny that Atlantis and Lemuria ever existed, open minded people are able to find a great deal of evidence which suggests that both of these "mythical" places did in fact exist.

The Greek "myth" of Atlantis has preserved the link between the modern world and the old. The story of Atlantis is part of our culture; since ancient times men have told the tale of Atlantis.

The Atlantic myth tells us that Atlantis was a great land, but due to a struggle between the forces of light and the forces of darkness, it was destroyed...engulfed by the ocean. But before its destruction great teachers carried its knowledge to many parts of the globe... The places that these teachers chose became the homes of modern civilizations.

Egypt, India, Mexico, and Tibet have legends which link their priesthood to Atlantis. Some say that Stonehenge and other monuments in the British Isles were constructed by Atlantians. The mysterious Druids of the British isles may be descendants of the Atlantians.

Languages which developed in Europe have very few words which use sound produced by the letter combination atl (the first syllable of the word Atlantis). While this may not seem very significant, some researchers point out that the fact that since the syllable atl is seldom used in European languages, it may indicate that the letter\sound unit atl is foreign to Europe.

In contrast to this, languages native to the Americas have many words which use the sound produced by the letters atl. Those who are given to speculation say that this may indicate that Atlantian culture did in fact exist, and that the Atlantians may be the ancestors of some, or all of the Native Americans.

In relation to these facts, it is interesting to note that Mexican nationals, and Spanish speaking Mexican Americans often refer to the southwestern region of the United States as Azatlan....

While many people have heard of Atlantis, the lost continent of Lemuria remains veiled in even deeper mystery. Certainly the best known source of information about Lemuria comes to us from the work of Colonel James Churchward.

Colonel Churchward was stationed in India around the turn of the century and had the opportunity to examine some of the oldest written records that have survived since the days before "history" began.

These ancient records told the story of an ancient land and civilization which had preceded civilization in India...The land of Mu, the Motherland, Lemuria.

Colonel Churchward's remarkable odyssey of discovery took him not only to one of the most secret places in India, but also to the site of an amazing archaeological find on the coast of Mexico. It was there that he found ancient tablets that were written in the same language which he had encountered in India.

These tablets told of the land of Mu and its religion. Colonel Churchward found the Lemurian religion to be so fascinating that he devoted an entire book just to that subject.

According to Colonel Churchward, our modern religions are a corruption of the Lemurian religion. He feels that each civilization that has fallen since the days of Lemuria has done so because the priesthood had created a power elite which led the people astray from the truth....

After studying the Mexican tablets, Colonel Churchward traveled around Central America and the southwestern United States studying native cultures. He discovered that the pueblo tribes of the southwest (Hopi, Pueblo, Zuni) use many of the same pictographic characters that Lemurians used, and he became convinced that these people were the descendants of the Lemurians.

The tribal legends of the Hopi Indians tell of a time when they fled their homeland and arrived here on this continent. What makes their history particularly interesting to modern Americans is the fact that the Hopis say that this is the fourth time they have migrated from a land that has been destroyed. And that this is the final round of their migrations, where the races will be either united, or destroyed.

Many Tribes in the North and Central American continents respect the Hopis as descendants of the old ones, and the keepers of the way.

The Hopis have preserved a prophecy for our times. The Hopis are keepers of ancient knowledge: They are the descendants of either the Lemurians, the Atlantians, or both. It is their tribal destiny to preserve a fragment of the ancient culture, so that we who live in these modern times will understand that the Human Race is much older than our priests tell us, and that our history is much different than our priests tell us.

Long before the first White Men ever set foot on this continent, the Hopis knew of their existence. The Hopi legends tell of a time when they were given the gift of Corn by the Goddess of the Earth. This Corn had kernels of four different colors: Red, Yellow, Black, and White. They were told that the four colors of their Corn stood for the four different races of men.

They were also told that the White Race would someday come. This would begin a time of trouble, because the White Race would not be in touch with the Earth, the Mother. Their legend tells that the White Race will defile the Earth and there will be a time of suffering for the Planet and its inhabitants. This will be a sign to the White Race: If they do not recognize the signs, correct their ways, and restore the balance, the Earth will "turn over" and get rid of us.

That is their way of saying the magnetic field of the Earth will shift, flipping the Earth over on its axis. This will cause volcanic eruptions, earthquakes, tidal waves, floods, etc. Science has proven that the Earth's magnetic field has indeed shifted many times....

Legends, and phantom memories of old Atlantis and Lemuria often present themselves to those who are in search of spiritual truth. A popular theory among metaphysically oriented people is that the mystery schools originated in Lemuria under the direction of extraterrestrial "deities" who represented the galactic brotherhood.

After the destruction of Lemuria, these mystery schools were carried to Atlantis. After the destruction of Atlantis, the keepers of the sacred mysteries migrated to Africa, the Mideast, the Far East, and to Central America, founding the schools of religious and scientific thought from which we draw our present day metaphysical knowledge and conventional religious thought.

As time separated the seekers of truth from the original teachings, these teachings gradually became distorted, yet each school of thought retained certain elements which lead modern thinkers to believe that **these systems have a common ancestor.**

We have explored the Atlantian and Lemurian myths, tracing them to the more current civilizations of the Mayans and the Hopis, because we must understand our magical heritage and recognize our path. We have strayed far from the truth and now it is time for us to return to the ways of the Earth.

Perhaps the best documented system for understanding our magical connection with the Earth comes to us from the teachings of Don Juan, as recorded in Carlos Castaneda's books. It should come as no surprise that Don Juan's lineage of Masters can be traced to the Mayans, perhaps originating in Lemuria.

When we compare Don Juan's teachings with those of other well known mystery teachings such as those of the Rosicrucians, we find many common elements including the belief in the Human Aura, the body of Light, astral projection, and the importance of dream work.

Don Juan told Carlos that the greatest love of the warrior was for the Earth. The warrior knows that we are all part of the Earth and that we draw our energy from the Earth.

Don Juan stated that the Earth has an energy field just as we do. We can use the energy of the Earth to alter our own energy fields, thus allowing us to experience other realities and transcend material existence.

He understood the fact that our planet is actually a spaceship which is traveling through a most amazing cosmos, and that when a person accepts the fact that they are a magical being, they are opening the door of limitless possibility.

The fact that these "secret" teachings have been revealed at this critical time in the course of Human evolution is a positive sign that we are heading in the right direction. Those who are attracted to these teachings, and who put them to work, are on the cutting edge of Human evolution.

It is interesting to note that certain prominent members of the metaphysical community believe that Mr. Castaneda's work has been a catalyst which brought metaphysical thought into the mainstream of the American consciousness.

THE MAYANS, MASTERS OF THE SPACE TIME ILLUSION

The rapid development of the Mayan culture and their advanced mathematical and astronomical sciences are evidence that they arrived in Central America as colonizers from an already advanced culture.

Before the arrival of the Spaniards, the Mayan culture was the most highly advanced society on this continent. There is evidence to suggest that the Mayan culture began as a Lemurian colony.

The last of the High Maya left this Planet before the Spanish arrived in Central America. They knew that this planet was entering one of its darkest periods and there was no need for them to attempt to overcome the densely material energies that this planet was about to experience.

The High Mayans are representatives of the Universal Priesthood, masters of the space-time illusion, capable of travelling throughout the galaxy by transmuting their bodies into vehicles of pure energy.

The Mayans understood the powers which create space by an instrument that records time, the Mayan Calendar. They knew that the Universe is a Hierarchy: Everything proceeds from the center of the Universe, the Infinite Source of Creation...the Godhead. The Mayans knew that on our level of existence we are not capable of perceiving the Infinite Source; we only know of it by its emanations, and that all phenomenon which we perceive is the result of these cosmic forces joining in unison to create the Universal Hologram, which is ruled by the laws of Mathematics, Geometry, and Music.

Many of the monuments that the Mayans left behind were recording instruments designed to calibrate Earth time to Galactic Synchronization. These monuments were built as a testament to future generations - that there is a Universal Truth greater than our Earthly illusion. And to serve as a link between intelligence on Earth, and that of the rest of the Galaxy.

The great stone monuments of the Mayans are like the monoliths of the motion picture *2001, A Space Odyssey*...The monuments of the Maya were left behind to serve as a sign for a future age: The time is right, EVOLVE.

We are now in the final twenty five year cycle of the Mayan Calendar. The evolution of the Planet, and its operators is accelerating at ever increasing rates.

This final twenty five year cycle began on August 17, 1987, the Harmonic Convergence. The next twenty five years will be the most exiting era this planet has known. It is time to open our minds and accept the information encoded in the Mayan calendar. The Universal Truths have not changed. The veil is lifting. It is time to let go of the ignorant beliefs that keep us from having the courage to perceive the truth.

The time has come for this planet and its inhabitants to evolve into the higher light realms. All signs say it is time and all systems are go. The materialists are in trouble. Everything is also the opposite of what it appears to be. The next stage of Human evolution is into the higher dimensional realms of light science. Those who base their existence on purely physical reality will have a hard time making the quantum leap into the new Solar Age.

THE
⊕ TROANO CODEX ⊕

A CRYPTIC MESSAGE FROM THE PAST

One of the most intriguing pieces of evidence which seems to indicate that Lemuria did indeed exist is an ancient Mayan codex (book) which refers to Lemuria directly.

This codex, the Troano codex, is known to be one of only three books which survived the destruction of the Aztec culture by the Spaniards.

The Troano codex is cataloged under the title the Madrid Codex, because it is now the property of the University of Madrid. Facsimile reproductions of this codex have been made with the cover title; the Madrid Codex (copyright 1939, the Maya Society, Baltimore Maryland). I have attempted to obtain this translation, but it is unavailable for inter-library loan.

This codex is mentioned in several books, including three classics in the field: *Sacred Mysteries of the Mayas and the Quiche, Maya/Atlantis Queen Moo and the Sphinx,* both by Le Plongeon, and in Churchward's; *the Lost Continent of MU.*

I would like to refer all who are interested in the Lemurian and Atlantian myths to these books and of course to the Troano Codex itself.

⊕ WHAT IS IN A NAME? ⊕

Sedona, we are told, is named after Sedona Schnebly, a woman of Pennsylvania Dutch descent.

Sedona Schnebly was born in the town of Gorin, Missouri in 1877. She came to the Sedona area in the year 1901, and by 1902, her name became the official name for the city of Red Hills.

History books tell us that no one in the Schnebly family is sure where the name Sedona came from. It appears to be an affectionate name that was "made up" by her parents....

It is a curious fact that the name Sedona is very similar in pronunciation to another name which appears at least twice in ancient tales of the Earth Goddess. This other name is pronounced; said-nuh, and can be spelled Sedna, or Seydna.

For those of us who are intrigued by the mysteries of life, and enjoy decoding its hidden messages, the name Sedna\Sedona offers a tantalizing clue about the true nature of the Spirit of this land.

While browsing through the bookstore one day, I was quite surprised to find a rather thought-provoking passage in the book titled *Christ Consciousness* (Norman Paulsen, Builders Press). The passage which caught my attention came from the Troano Codex. This passage referred to a Lemurian Earth Goddess whose name is pronounced; said-nuh, and spelled Seydna.

This Lemurian Goddess myth offers an interesting clue to those who seek to substantiate the Lemuria/Sedona connection, and understand the true significance of the Vortex phenomenon.

Several months before I read this passage in *Christ Consciousness*, I met a interesting individual, Mr. Jade Wah'oo, who is of both Mongolian and Native American descent. He had come to Sedona with a very old Mongolian tale of an Earth Goddess who would someday be found in a castle made of red rock. Her name is Sedna (pronounced said-nuh). Mr. Wah'oo believes that Sedona is the place where this Goddess will be found.

Those who allow themselves to believe the Hopi Indian migration myths should have no trouble accepting the notion that the Mongol tribes of central Asia may have also descended from Lemurian colonists. If we can accept the idea that the Mongols are indeed descended from the Lemurians, it should then come as no surprise to us that their tale of Sedna could actually be based upon ancient Lemurian teachings.

THE WAY OF THE MEDICINE WHEEL

We are being drawn together in the Medicine Wheel so that we can combine our energies for the healing of the Planet Earth. The Solstices, Equinoxes, and times of the full Moon are very important times to get in touch with the energies of the Earth through the Medicine Wheel. Always plan a celebration for these times (weather permitting). People all over the planet use these "Solar" and "Lunar" holidays as times of thanks and celebration. You can be sure that on these special days you will be joining your energies together with millions of people who are celebrating the same thing at the same time planet wide.

The art and practice of Geomantic ritual may include observations of heavenly bodies. The Magic Circle can serve as an observatory and a calendar whose perimeter is used to mark the passages of the Sun, the Moon and the Stars. Stonehenge is an excellent example of this. Building a Wheel which marks the transit of the heavenly bodies is an act of magic.

THE MEDICINE WHEEL
GEOMANTIC EARTH HEALING CEREMONIES

This is not meant to be a teaching of Native American ways. I am not an Indian; I am of European descent. It is not appropriate for me to set myself up as a teacher of Native American ways. What must be understood is that these teachings are for every Tribe. This is the Rainbow path. Black Elk, the great Sioux Indian warrior and teacher, had a powerful vision in which he saw that all groups of people will someday come together within "The Sacred Hoop of the Nations." the Medicine Wheel.

Every person who reads this book knows that this planet and its occupants are currently going through a very critical phase of accelerated evolution.

⊕ CHILDHOOD'S END ⊕

A vision has been given to many of us, telling us that it is time to bond our energies together in prayer and ceremony to create an energy field that will stabilize our planet and bring peace to the hearts of Men.

It is time for those of us who can hear the call to establish an energy network (Web) of Medicine Wheels around the globe. By bonding our energies together in ceremony we will create a powerful energy field which will affect the group consciousness of humanity.

The word "medicine" as it is used in the term Medicine Wheel actually means magic. Every Human Being is a magical being in a magical Universe; everything is a miracle. To know God and be self aware is an act of magic. All religion is magic.

In the world of the native shaman, medicine/healing and magic are one thing...They are both directly related to our ability to purify, focus, and control our personal energy fields.

The Medicine Wheel is a magical circle of power. By properly conducting a ceremony we can influence the energy pattern of the Universe.

The resonant form of the Medicine Wheel serves to focus and amplify the combined energies of the group of people that are conducting the ceremony. Group meditations and visualizations done within the Medicine Wheel can affect planetary destiny. **(Remember that through the power of the Human Will we have the ability to control the forces which create our world. Everything is energy; by Willing things to happen, they can become reality.)**

Specific leaders, or problem areas can be "targeted" to receive the healing of the Wheel. Ceremonies may be held for the express purpose of calling rain into an area, or for projecting healing energies into the Earth Mother.

When using these powers it is important to remember that it is bad karma to command people to do things against their Will. If someone such as a national leader is doing something you do not like, don't risk performing a meditation or ceremony commanding them to stop. Doing so will result in a dangerous Karmic backlash. If you want someone to change their ways send them love....

102

A FEW NOTES ABOUT MEDICINE WHEELS
⊕　　　AND CEREMONY　　　⊕

The rules of ceremony vary from Tribe to Tribe, and it seems that no matter how one performs their ceremony there is always someone else who thinks it should be done a different way. So instead of giving a detailed dogmatic description of ceremony, let us just touch on a few of the basics.

When we enter the Wheel we do it with the intent of performing a ceremony. The act of entering the Wheel separates us from our daily routine and ordinary reality. When you enter the Wheel you are in a magical space: It is the temple of God and Goddess, the Universal Mind of the I AM presence.

Look inside yourself and find the Truth of your Heart. Use your prayers to give that truth back to the Universe...the Great Spirit. Find a quiet place inside your being and send out healing love to all in your circle.

At the beginning of each ceremony a prayer should always be directed to the Great Spirit, the Four Directions, the Father (the Sun), and the Mother (the Earth). [Each Tribe has different names for these entities, so you should use whatever names you feel most comfortable with.]

The tradition which I am familiar with begins with a prayer giving thanks and then asking for guidance, protection and blessings, first from the Great Spirit, and then the Four Directions, beginning with the East then moving around the Wheel in a clockwise direction, to the South, the West, and then the North. [Each tribe, has different names for these entities, so you should use whatever names you feel most comfortable with.] After prayers have been given to the directions, the Father (the Sun), and the Mother (the Earth) are honored.

After the opening prayers it is often a good idea to play drums, chant, or sing, in order for the group energy to become unified and harmonious.

Each person who wants to should have a chance to give a short prayer from their heart. If the group enjoys drumming etc. another period of music may follow the prayers.

While people are "up" and the energy is high, it is time to conduct a guided light meditation which invokes the light of Christ to fill the participants' hearts and all others across the planet.

Advanced groups can create strong Vortices of energy by standing on the edge of the Wheel facing the center and visualizing energy swirling around the Wheel from the right to the left. (Which is clockwise.)

After the initial invocation of light, specific people or places etc. should be focused upon to receive love and healing.

These ceremonies should not be used to command people against their will. This would be an improper use of Will, service to the self which will ultimately result in bad Karma for those who work the ceremony.

Love conquers all. Love heals all wounds. Send out only love.

⊕ PRAY FOR WORLD PEACE, AND HEALING ⊕

The goal is to project healing and centering energies into the energy field of the Earth. The Earth hears, and responds to our prayers.

These ceremonies have the power to affect the "group consciousness"of our fellow Human Beings.

By working Medicine Wheel Ceremonies, we are able to reach the hearts of Humanity directly, on a level which is beyond words or thought; the inner planes of the magical reality.

⊕ ⊕ ⊕

Oh Great Spirit please hear my prayer, I am praying for our Mother, the Earth. Please send her your blessings and your healing light.

I say a prayer for the rainforests.

In the name of the Great Spirit, I call out to those who are in positions of power, in government, and in business. I specifically send my prayers to those who can directly affect the destiny of the rainforests. I call out to them to open their eyes and see what they are doing to the planet.

I pray that the Great Spirit will make them aware that they have to start taking action to save the rainforest NOW. I pray that the Great Spirit will make these leaders aware of alternative ways of thought and action.

I pray that the World Bank will not finance any more hydroelectric projects or logging roads in Central or South American countries.

I say a prayer for the world leaders. May they find the way of peace. I invoke the light of Christ to surround these beings and fill them with the cleansing and purifying light of Christ's love. I specifically say a prayer for Mr. Gorbachev. May Christ be with him and may he be blessed and protected.

I say a prayer for Mr. Bush. May Christ be with him and may he be blessed and protected. May he have the wisdom to be a truly wise man.

⊕ ⊕ ⊕

With the Energy of our prayers we help to soften the hearts of our fellow beings. We help them see a new way of living which is beyond fear, greed, and hatred.

Powerful Universal forces which we can barely comprehend are opening up the energy centers of Men and Women around the planet. The every person is ready to receive new information and let go of old programs. The winds of change are blowing.

OUR PRAYERS HELP OUR FELLOW HUMAN BEINGS SEE THAT
THEY CAN BREAK TRADITION!
THEY DO NOT HAVE TO FOLLOW THE WAYS OF HATRED.

Selecting a proper site is important, but it is not always necessary to find a place that is already a place of power. Human Beings are able to draw Power into a place, thus 'creating' a Power Spot. You can build a Medicine Wheel in your backyard, and if it is used regularly for prayer, meditation, and ceremony, it will become a Power Spot, a Wheel within a Wheel in the Web of Life.

When you start looking for a place to build a Wheel, ask yourself and your friends if they know about any places nearby in the country that are known as a Power Spots. Follow your heart, and remember that people are drawn to Power Spots naturally. Choose a place, and bless it with prayers.

Any time you start a Wheel, it is important to bless the sacred ground with prayers. Being sure to banish undesirable energy from the area by invoking the power of the Great Spirit and the presence of Christ.

Native Americans recommend burning sage as an incense to drive out 'bad' spirits. If available liberal amounts of sage smoke should be applied to all participants in the ceremony, and to the sacred space itself.

Driving a stake in the ground to mark the center of the sacred ground is the first ritual of the Wheel, symbolizing the descent of Spirit into matter and marking the center of the sacred ground.

After that, tie a string or a rope to the center stake, and scribe a circle on the Earth, thus establishing the boundary of the sacred ground.

Aligning your Wheel with a magnetic compass is the easiest way to find the Four Directions. We know that true North (geographically) is not magnetic North. But if your Wheel is aligned with the magnetic field of the Earth you can be sure that you are resonating with the Planetary Grid.

Ancient Geomancers would mark the cardinal points by observing the shadow cast by the center pole as the Sun rose and set on the days of the equinox. The North and South points can then be determined by dividing the circle between the East and West points, or by using the North Star.

Medicine Wheels are usually built out of stone and left intact after the ceremony, permanently marking the area as a sacred spot. However, it is not always necessary to build a Medicine Wheel with physical objects such as stones, and sometimes, particularly in city situations, building a stone circle can be very impractical and even undesirable. (You never know who may come along and desecrate the temple.) Powerful energy fields can be raised just by gathering a group of people together in a circle with ceremonial intent. PERMANENT AR-CHITECTURE IS UNNECESSARY. Crystals, or other special rocks or objects can be carried to ceremonies, and then returned home with their keepers.

As the global village develops and we are able to learn and compare the customs, beliefs, and rituals of groups of people (Tribes) around the world, we find that some few things remain constant and that many things differ.

While doing research for this book I discovered that native people around the world teach of the Sacred Wheel and the Four Directions. These teachings are Universal; however, the way these things are interpreted tends to vary according to the position of the observers, and the way they interpret reality.

Native people know that the circle is the sacred form of creation. They are able to observe that all things occur in cycles (circles). The circular form represents the womb, from which all life proceeds. It symbolizes motherhood, and is known to be the form of the Mother Earth, whom all native people hold in deep respect.

The Four Directions are universal archetypes. They define the void of the cosmic egg. We can only try to understand them with the perceptions we are given, and our perceptions are limited to the definitions created by our reality tunnels.

Each Tribe has its own language and therefore its own names for these Spirit beings. Western mystics call them Archangels... The Most High Servants of the Great Spirit.

When Native American teachers speak of these Spirits in English, they usually refer to them as "Grandfathers." This term denotes a great deal of respect for these Spirit beings, and it also helps to let us know that our world is woven from the Spirit of these great beings that has descended through the levels of existence....

Each Tribe "creates" a mandala of the Universe which is a projection of their individual way of seeing things. All names, attributes, colors etc. which are used to describe the directions are merely illusions of the absolute reality..

> *There is evidence to suggest that the teaching of the Wheel and the Four Directions, Geomancy, and Earth worship were handed down from prehistory civilizations such as Atlantis or Lemuria.*

The teachings of the Wheel vary from Tribe to Tribe. It may be impossible to tell which Tribe carries the true teaching, and which other Tribes have distorted the ancient teachings to suit their own perceptions.According to the Hopi and the Mayan traditions the colors of the directions of the are as follow:

NORTH....... WHITE

EAST................. RED

SOUTH.....YELLOW

WEST.......... BLACK

Most Tribes in North America also think of White as being the color for North, and Black as being the color for West. However, among the American Tribes there is a definite difference of opinion about which colors should be used to represent South and East.

Black Elk says that his people think of the South being a place of red Earth and heat, so it should be represented with the color Red. And that as the place where the Sun rises, East should definitely be represented by the color Yellow.

Hymenyhosts Storm, author of the powerful book *Seven Arrows*, says that his people think of South as being a place where there is an abundance of plant life, so it should be represented by the color Green.

My Tribe, my English speaking ancestors, whose mystic traditions have their roots in the Hermetic teachings of ancient Egypt (which some claim were handed down directly from the Atlantians), call the Four Directions Archangels, and know them by the names: Michael, Auriel, Raphael, and Gabriel. The power, color, and position of these great beings are as follows:

RAPHAEL	EAST	YELLOW	AIR	(SPACE)
MICHAEL	SOUTH	RED	FIRE	(ENERGY)
GABRIEL	WEST	BLUE	WATER	(MOVEMENT)
AURIEL	NORTH	BLACK	EARTH	(MATTER)

Notice that black is the color of the Northern quadrant. This is because the Hermetic teachings say that the energy field of the Earth travels from the South to the North... The North is the place of darkness and finality...the Sun rests in a field of Blue.

THREE DIMENSIONAL SPACE TIME

Physicists believe that all energy and matter in our Universe operate in a "unified field" which can be understood in the terms as the interaction of four basic forces:

Gravity

Electromagnetism

Weak Force (radiational)

Strong Force (sub atomic)

DIRECTION IS RELATIVE TO THE
POSITION OF THE OBSERVER

The way of the Sun is "clockwise". Generally speaking, when we perform Medicine Wheel ceremonies or otherwise invoke the"spiritual whirlwind." It is safest to work with this side of Spirit.

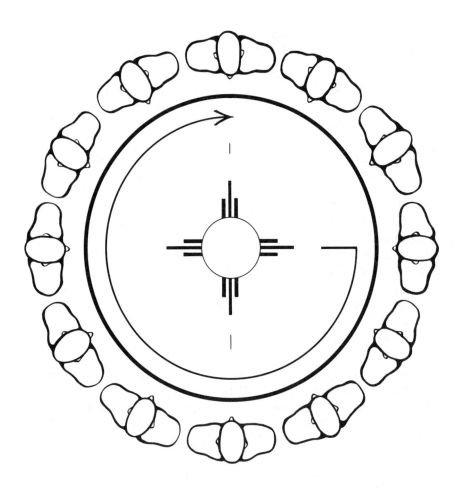

Notice that as you change position in a Vortex such as Medicine Wheel, from the center (looking out) to the edge looking in, the clockwise energy flow appears to move past you in opposite directions. From left to right in the center, and right to left on the edge (looking in).

UNDERSTANDING THE TWIN
SPIRALS OF LIFE

The level of reality on which we exist is one of duality: all things exist in a positive and negative state, the proverbial Yin and the Yang.

We know not where the twin spirals of intergalactic intelligence originate, but on every level we are able to explore we see this twin spiral pattern of creative force. From the double helix of the DNA molecule to the spiral form of the galaxies, we see the cosmic blueprint of positive and negative spiral wave forms.

The term "twin spirals" does not mean that these two forces are exactly alike; in fact, they are exactly un-alike. Each is the mirror image of its counterpart, and the exact complement to its qualities. The twin spirals are always in balance; they are one.

The only reference points we have for understanding which of the twin spirals we are working with are our physical body and our planet.

As we stand upon the Earth the flow of cosmic energy which we consider positive (descending upon us from Spirit) is the energy whose motion we perceive as flowing in a clockwise direction into the Earth.

This means that if were standing in the **center** of a Medicine Wheel or Vortex this energy would be flowing around us from left to right in front of us, and from right to left behind us.

However, during many types of ceremonies we stand on the **outside** of a Medicine Wheel facing its center. In this case the clockwise energy flow would be moving in front of us from right to left. (Notice how direction appears to change in relation to our position.)

Beginners should practice working with the energy which is moving in a clockwise direction because it is this energy which cleanses and recharges our Aura. It also carries Spiritual force from the higher planes that inspires the mind.

When we have gathered around the Medicine Wheel, we should use our Will and our power of creative visualization to focus a spiral Vortex of energy which moves in a clockwise direction into the Earth. This exercise heals both the planet and those who are working the ceremony.

To do this the group faces the center of the Wheel with their right hands placed (palm down) over their partner's left hands (palm up), as their Will is used to invoke the spiral flow of energy from right to left around the circle.

Advanced students and groups can use the counterclockwise flow of energy to invoke the forces of nature to alter reality. This flow of energy ascends from matter to Spirit. The danger of working with this side of the Force is that it is tainted with the dense material vibrations of matter.

The only way to overcome the negative aspect of the counterclockwise energy is to let only love guide your thoughts and actions. Never use your power to command people against their Will. If you want someone to change, send them love.

Project only Love, and healing light.

Many of you are familiar with the rose and the cross design, which is said to come from the ancient Egyptians. The rose and the cross design has many meanings. In a few words, it can be said that the rose is a symbol of life and consciousness arising from the union of the forces of creation. This union is Love on the cosmic scale. It is represented to us by the cross, the symbol of Love and Christ energy....

The circle was chosen as the shape for Earth Temples because our ancestors knew that was the shape of the Mother, and that all things in nature occur in cycles (circles).

Modern Geomancers will tell you that the circle is chosen because it is a resonant form. The circle relates symbolically and mathematically to the form and order of the Universe.

Mathematic ratios based upon the circle define the growth patterns and perfect spiral forms of natural creation found throughout the observable Universe. Many ancient temples, such as the ones built by the Greeks, as well as many Christian cathedrals, are designed using ratios taken from the form of the circle....

The "empty" circle symbolizes the infinite void of the cosmic egg, being pure potential and undifferentiated form. This is the mathematical figure Zero, which represents the void from which all things proceed.

The center point within the circle represents the Great Spirit, the mind of God, the original cause which organized the formless void of the cosmic egg into form.

The vertical line descending, represents the male (electrical) force of creation making the descent of Spirit into matter. This is the numeral ONE, the first unit to separate itself from the void.

The horizontal line represents the female (magnetic) aspect of creation, which is receiving.

The cross represents interweaving of forces that unite to form the physical universe. It is the union of the male and the female energies otherwise known as Love.

GOD IS AN INTELLIGENT SPHERE WHOSE CENTER IS EVERYWHERE, AND WHOSE CIRCUMFERENCE IS NOWHERE.
(Hermes Trismegistus)

What is the difference between White magic and Black magic? Think about what the following statement tells us.

The Law of One states that there are but two paths; service to others, and service to self. Service to others is the way of love, and service to self is the way of slavery.

SUGGESTED READING

In order that we may help those who quest for knowledge the Vortex Society offers a mail order book service.

Please write for our free catalogue and newsletter.

Stay in touch with the magic of Sedona.

SHAMANISM HEALING MAGIC SCIENCE
SEDONA

ANCIENT WISDOM
Christ Consciousness. Norman Paulsen
Color Meditations. S.J.G. Ousely (Classic)
Earth Magic. Marion Weinstein
The Finding of the Third Eye. Vera Stanley Alder
The Keys of Enoch. J.J. Hurtak
The Kybalion. Three Initiates
Rainbow Bridge. Three Disciples
The Secret Doctrine. H.P. Blavatsky (Classic)
The Seven Mansions of Color. Alex Jones (Color Meditation)
Shamanism for the New Age. Jan Hartman N.D., P.H.D.
The Way of the Shaman. Michael Harner
Books by C.C. Zain. From the Brotherhood of Life, P.O. Box 76862 LA, CA, 90076

CRYSTALS DOWSING AND RADIONICS
Beyond Pendulum Power, Entering the Energy World. Grey Nielsen
The Complete Crystal Guidebook. Uma Silbey
The Crystal Connection. Randal N. Baer, Vicki Baer
Radionics, Science of Magic. David Tansley D. C.
Ray Paths and Chakra Gateways. David Tansley D.C.
Spiritual Dowsing. Sid Lonegren (Classic)

EARTH ENERGY
Earth Energy. J. Havelock Fidler
Feng Shui. Ernest J. Eitel (Classic)

LIFE FORCE ENERGY
Awakening Healing Energy Through the Tao. Mantak Chia, Michael Winn (Destined to become a classic)
Biocircuits, Amazing New Tools for Energy Health. Leslie and Terry Patten
The Body Electric, Electromagnetism and the Foundation of Life. Gary Selden
The Lakhovsky Multiple Wave Oscillator. Edited by Tom Brown - Borderland Research Foundation. P.O. Box 429, Garberville CA 95440
Pyramid Energy, the Philosophy of God, the Science of Man. Hardy, Hardy, Killock, Killock (Excellent)
Subtle Energy. John Davidson

Vibrational Medicine. Richard Gerber. (Excellent)
The Web of Life. John Davidson (Electromagnetic!)
Wheels of Life, a users guide to the Chakra System. Anodea Judith
Wheels of Light. Rosalyn l. Bruyere, Jeanne Farrens
Wilhelm Reich-The Evolution of His Work. David Boadella (Wilhelm Reich was perhaps the first modern scientist to propose that "Life Force Energy" existed....Fascinating)

NATIVE AMERICAN WISDOM AND LEGENDS
Black Elk Speaks. John G. Neihardt (Classic)
Book of the Hopi. Frank Waters
Cuchama and Sacred Mountains. Evens Wentz
The Lost Continent of Mu. Colonel James Churchward
The Medicine Wheel. Earth Astrology, Sun Bear, and Wabun
The Warriors of the Rainbow. William Willoya, and Vinson Brown
The Way of the Sun. White Eagle

PSYCHOLOGY AND THE MAGIC OF THE MIND
Creative Visualization. Shakti Gawain
The Dream Illuminati. Wayne Saalman
Programming and Metaprogramming the Human Biocomputer. John Lilly
Prometheus Rising. Robert Anton Wilson
Right Use of Will. and Earth Spell. Ceanne DeRohan - 535 Cordova rd. #112, Santa Fe, New Mexico 87501
The Tibetan Book of the Dead. Evens Wentz (Classic)
What Does WoMan Want? Timothy Leary (the Former Harvard Professor is Quite Wise)
Zen Mind Beginners Mind. D.T. Suzuki (Classic)

SCIENCE FICTION
Childhoods End. Arthur C. Clarke (Classic)

TAPPING INTO THE UNIVERSAL ENERGY FIELD FOR "FREE" ENERGY
Anti Gravity and the World Grid. David Hatcher Childress
Tapping Zero Point Energy. Moray B. King
Handbook of Unusual Energies. Jerry Gallimore - C.A. Dake Industries. p.o. box 1866, Clayton, Georgia 30525

UFO'S
Cosmic Trigger, the Final Secret of the Illuminati. Robert Anton Wilson
The Prism of Lyra, An Exploration of Human Galactic Heritage. Lyssa Royal, Keith Priest
The RA Material. Don Elkins, Carla Rueckert, James Allen Mcarty
Uri: A Journal of the Mystery of Uri Geller. Andrija Puharich. (Interesting information about UFO'S)

Most of the books listed here are available through the Vortex Society.